Merle's KITCHEN

Merle's KITCHEN

Merle Parrish

To my family

Introduction	vii
Merle's Baking Hints	xii
Cakes	1
Sponges	49
Puddings and desserts	65
Biscuits and cookies	97
Slices	127
Morning and afternoon tea	171
Scones	209
Acknowledgements	221
Index	222

Contents

[*Top*] Clyde, me and the wedding party, 23 January 1954 [*Middle*] My sister Enid (5 years) me (3 years) and my brother Albert (7 years) [*Bottom*] Me at 16 years old [*Opposite*] Me and Clyde on our wedding

Introduction

In the big towns there are bakers' shops and you can buy cakes and slices and scones. It's not the same in the country. There's no bakery in the village of Cudal in NSW, where I live. There are only 400 people and if you want cake you have to make your own. I started baking when I was seven years old. My mother was a good cook and I was the only daughter and would help her in the kitchen. We had a big kitchen — not like my small kitchen now — and there was a big table in the middle. The kitchen was the heart of the home in those days.

My first attempt at baking was a batch of Anzac biscuits. I then started making patty cakes in little patty papers when I was nine. I have always liked things that are nice to eat and fattening, and I found I could cook them better than other people. I won my first competition with my Anzac biscuits when I was seven and won my first prize for cake baking in the junior section for my patty cakes in the local show. Right from the start I loved the competitive atmosphere at the local shows. Over the years I've been fortunate to win hundreds of prizes, but I don't mind when I'm beaten fairly.

Mind you, not all my attempts were successful. When I was in my early teens and still getting into baking, I made my father a batch of scones to have when he came home. My mother was away, so she wasn't there to guide me. Those scones were awful. They were so hard. I threw one up in the air and it lobbed on a chook!

After I left school I was a telephonist at the local post office and that's where I met Clyde Parrish. We were married on 23 January 1954. I was 21 and he was 32. I soon had three kids under three: David was born in 1955, Marianne in 1957 and Robert in 1958. Thankfully I had a wonderful mother to help.

When the kids were young I was always cooking and baking. I made batches of biscuits for the kids (and their friends), there was cake every week and I made pudding with the main meal every single day. Clyde had a beautiful flower and vegie garden and we enjoyed plenty of fresh vegies.

Just as my mother guided me in the kitchen, so I guided my kids. They all loved it. I set up a little stool so they could stand at the table. They would make a big mess, but it didn't matter. Later I introduced a rule: whoever was baking would have to clean up afterwards for the next one's turn.

I was always active in the Country Women's Association (CWA) and I was baking for competitions and social events all the time. Clyde would help me. He would stand and wash up for hours. I was making and icing the same sorts of cakes at home that I would enter into competitions at the shows – it was just a habit. The kids also entered cookery competitions. When Marianne was 11 years old, she asked me if she could enter a chocolate cake in the junior section of *The Land* Cookery Competition, which is a state competition. She made it 90 per cent on her own, and lo and behold, she won. In 2011 we were told by *The Land* newspaper that Marianne's win all those years ago could be found in the archives of the newspaper.

Most families do like chocolate cake. I don't like eating cake that much and chocolate cake is difficult to get right. If the ingredients aren't balanced it can be soggy and sink in the middle. It was a great honour therefore to win the inaugural Donna Latter Memorial Trophy for Supreme Chocolate Cake, which was introduced as a special category in *The Land* Cookery Competition when Donna died suddenly. I still get a thrill now when I talk about the win.

In 1988 I took the next progression and completed my CWA Judges' Certificate. When I took the exam, 32 people applied and 14 passed, so it was reasonably tough. I've been judging now for more than 30 years and I always enjoy it, always find it interesting. When you test a cake, you taste a small, triangular piece and you test for how fine the mixture is, if it's soggy or sticky or overcooked or undercooked, as well as its general appearance and presentation.

The main thing when it comes to baking is to know your stove. Timing is also important. I always assemble my ingredients and grease and flour the tin before I start. This is partly because of lack of bench space. I have to keep things tidy as I go, and when I was on *MasterChef* everyone commented on how neat I was. It also helps me to get the timing right. I measure my ingredients carefully. In the old days, we used scales with weights. We had to do everything by hand, but now I can use my Mixmaster. And I use salted butter. A little bit of salt brings out the flavour in everything.

MasterChef was a wonderful experience. The producers rang the Central Western Group President of the CWA, Mrs Gail Hayden, looking for someone to appear on the show in a baking challenge, and Gail gave them my name. I think the young guy who I competed against, Billy, was flabbergasted to be challenged to bake a cake from a handwritten recipe. I gave him my recipe and he was thrilled to have it. The judges and everyone at *MasterChef* were very helpful, everyone was very nice. I never would have believed I'd be involved in something like that.

My kids have been telling me I should do a cookery book for years. All my recipes are in my head, and some of those are my mother's and some are my grandmother's. My son David said to me, 'If you fall off the perch, Mum, there will be no recipes.' So, the experience of *MasterChef* encouraged me to finally write a book. It was difficult to get the recipes down and make them clear so another person could follow them. But they are all made with simple ingredients that most people would have in the pantry already – sugar, butter, flour, eggs. None of them are hard to do or expensive.

[*Top*] Clyde and me on the dance floor at our daughter Marianne and Peter's wedding in 1993 [*Middle and bottom*] Me hard at work in the kitchen

I have been a member of the CWA for 58 years now and I would hate not to be involved. People think of it as being nothing but tea and scones, but we do a lot of work that people don't see. We give back to the community; and the friendships I have had there over the years are unreal. Clyde was a very active man and between us we were members of 20 organisations in our district. We were both awarded Citizens Awards: me in 1990, and Clyde in 1996. He passed away on 13 June 2010 and I miss him. I'm still busy; it gets me out to help people and be social. You get housebound and stale if you don't do things.

I'm a life member of our local show, which has been going now for 110 years. I'm still baking for competitions and shows. People say to me, 'You're mad', but I love doing it. When I do the Sydney Royal Easter Show – now, don't laugh at what I'm about to say – I get up at 2 am to bake at least three batches of scones and a sponge roll. I leave at 5 am and my friend Margaret and I are in Orange at 6 am to catch the coach down to Sydney. Margaret has been a wonderful friend and neighbour to Clyde and me for many years, and especially since Clyde passed away.

I'm good with my hands. I've won many prizes for my knitting and my flower arranging, though not as many as I've won for my baking. I taught cake decorating for 25 years. One of my students, Kellie, who was 10 when she started learning from me, is now a teacher herself. Some of her students recently won a competition at our local show.

It's lovely to share things that you're good at. The only thing I won't share is my husband! But I have never not given a recipe to someone who wanted it. I love to share what I have perfected over the years, what I know and my philosophy of life. That's what I'm sharing with you now in this book.

Merle Parrish

Merle's baking hints

You may not be cooking to win a gold medal, but having a few hints and tips to help you along will ensure your baked goodies look and taste great!

- Always preheat the oven well before you want to start cooking. This guarantees that your cake will go into the oven at the correct temperature and begin to bake immediately.

- If using a fan-forced oven, reduce the given temperature by 20°C. If you are cooking on two shelves (for example, two trays of biscuits), swap them halfway through so they cook evenly. This doesn't apply to fan-forced ovens, where the temperature is more even throughout the oven.

- Prepare your tins, either by greasing and/or lining, before you start. That way you won't have to leave your uncooked mixture sitting around while you hunt for the tin you need.

- When I buy a new tin I never use it straight away. First I put the empty tin in the oven on a high temperature for 30 minutes. Doing this means that when you start to use it, the mixture doesn't stick to the sides.

- Use the tin size asked for in the recipe. If the tin is too small, your cake may overflow, making a mess. Too big and the cake might not be nice and high. Don't overcrowd biscuits on a baking tray, as they often need room to spread. Measure tins across the base for accuracy.

- The traditional way to prepare a tin was to grease it well with butter, then to dust with a light coating of flour. These days you can use a lining of baking paper, a non-stick product available from the supermarket. Grease the tin first so the paper sticks and doesn't slide about when you fill the tin.

- When creaming butter and sugar, make sure you do it long enough so it becomes very pale – almost white – and the sugar dissolves into the butter.

- Once flour is added to a mixture, treat it very gently. Overworking a flour mixture can mean your cake, biscuits or pastry become tough and even misshapen when cooked. Use a large metal spoon or a spatula to fold flour into a cake batter, and use a butter knife in a cutting motion to mix flour into a biscuit or pastry dough.
- I always use white sugar, but you could use caster sugar if you like.
- To test if your cake is cooked, give a gentle press in the centre. If it springs back, it is done. Cool your cake in the tin for a few minutes before turning out onto a wire rack. Cool completely before you top with an icing.
- Store leftover goodies in an airtight container in a cool, dark place.
- When cooking for competitions I never use a wire rack to cool my recipes after they have been in the oven as it leaves marks on the cakes, slices, biscuits and scones. Instead, you can use a plain tea towel with newspaper underneath. This will stop the marks.

I use large (59g) eggs

I use standard metric measuring cups and spoons.

1 tbsp = 20ml, 1 tsp = 5ml

All cup and spoon measures are level, unless otherwise stated.

OVEN TEMPERATURES

Very slow (100°–120°C) (215°–250°F)

Slow (145°–150°C) (290°–300°F)

Moderately slow (160°C) (315°F)

Moderate (170°–180°C) (325°–350°F)

Moderately hot (190°–200°C) (375°–400°F)

Hot (220°C) (425°F)

SOME SIMPLE CONVERSIONS

30g	–	1 oz
250g	–	8 oz
500g	–	1 lb
1kg	–	2 lb
30ml	–	1 fl oz
125ml	–	4 fl oz – ½ cup
250ml	–	8 fl oz – 1 cup
5mm	–	¼ inch
1cm	–	½ inch
3cm	–	1¼ inch
18cm	–	7 inch
20cm	–	8 inch
30cm	–	12 inch

Cakes

I first made patty cakes in little patty papers when I was about nine years old, still very young. I didn't make my first big cake until I was 16, one layer with icing. ❁ For shows, the judges request a plain icing because fancy decoration causes issues when cutting. The secret of even icing is to place it in the middle of the cake while the icing is still warm and spread it out quickly. I make my edge with my grandmother's bone-handled palette knife, but you could use a spatula just as well.

Sultana cake

PREP TIME: 30 MINS
COOKING TIME: 2 HOURS
SERVES 12

400g sultanas
½ cup brandy
1 cup water
2 tsp cornflour
250g butter, at room temperature, chopped
1 cup white sugar
3 eggs
2 cups plain flour
1 tsp baking powder

A great standby cake to have in the house, as you can keep it for days.

1 Preheat the oven to moderately slow (140°C). Grease a 22cm (base measurement) round cake tin, and line the base with baking paper.

2 Combine the sultanas, brandy and half the water in a saucepan. Bring to the boil over medium-low heat and simmer until the liquid has absorbed into the fruit.

3 Stir the cornflour and remaining water together until smooth and add to the pan. Stir for 2–3 minutes, until it comes to the boil and thickens. Remove from the heat, cover the surface with cling film and leave to cool until just lukewarm.

4 Use electric beaters to cream the butter and sugar until white and fluffy. Add the eggs one at a time, beating well after each addition. Fold in the sifted flour and baking powder, then the sultana mixture. Spoon into the tin, and smooth the surface. Bake for 2 hours, on the second bottom shelf of your oven, until firm to a gentle touch in the centre. Cool in the tin for 15 minutes, then turn out onto a wire rack to cool completely.

Peach blossom cake

PREP TIME: 30 MINS
COOKING TIME: 70 MINS
SERVES 8

This is the cake I want to dedicate to my best mate Clyde. It also won me enough points on MasterChef to help me claim the immunity pin!

190g butter, at room temperature, chopped
1¼ cups white sugar
¾ cup milk
1 tsp vanilla essence
1½ cups plain flour
¾ cup cornflour
1½ tsp baking powder
pinch of salt
6 egg whites
1–2 drops rose pink food colouring

ICING
1½ cups icing sugar
10g butter
2 tbsp boiling water
few drops of rose pink food colouring

NOTE: If you can't get the 20cm round deep tin, try this in a regular 22cm round tin instead.

1. Preheat the oven to slow (150°C). Grease a 20cm (base measurement) round, deep cake tin (see note). Line the base with baking paper.

2. Cream the butter and sugar in the small bowl of an electric mixer until white and fluffy. Gradually add half the milk to help dissolve the sugar, and beat well. Beat in the vanilla. Transfer to a larger bowl.

3. Sift the flour, cornflour, baking powder and salt together 3 times. Fold into the butter mixture, then add remaining milk (don't worry if it appears curdled at this stage). In another bowl, use clean beaters to beat the egg whites to stiff peaks. Fold half the egg whites into the cake batter, then fold in remaining egg whites.

4. Transfer 1 cup of the mixture to a smaller bowl, and stir in 1–2 drops food colouring. Take about ¾ cup of the white mixture, and spread over the base of the tin. Take half the pink batter, and spoon it in a ring about 1cm in from the tin edge – it should be about 1–1.5cm wide.

5. Very carefully spread half the remaining white batter over, taking care not to disturb the pink ring. Spoon the remaining pink batter into the centre of the tin, making about an 8cm round. Spoon the remaining white batter over the whole top, again taking care not to disturb the pink round.

6. Bake for about 70 minutes, until the cake is springy to a gentle touch in the centre and comes away from the sides of the tin. It may appear slightly cracked in the centre, but will settle flat on cooling. (If not, gently press the top flat with your fingertips.) Turn out onto a clean tea towel lined with a sheet of baking paper. Leave to cool.

7. To make the icing, combine the ingredients until smooth. Spread over the top of the cooled cake, and leave to set.

Apple cake

PREP TIME: 20 MINS
COOKING TIME: 50–60 MINS
SERVES 8–10

1½ cups wholemeal self-raising flour
1 tsp ground cinnamon
1 cup brown sugar
1 cup sultanas or dried mixed fruit
2 eggs, lightly beaten
2 tbsp vegetable oil
½ cup milk
2 apples, peeled, cored, thinly sliced
honey, to drizzle, optional

1 Preheat oven to moderate (180°C). Grease a 20cm (base measurement) square or round cake tin and line the base with baking paper, hanging over two sides.

2 Sift the flour and cinnamon into a mixing bowl and return the husks. Stir in the sugar and sultanas and make a well in the centre.

3 Add the eggs, oil and milk, and gently fold together. Pour into the tin and smooth the surface. Scatter the apple on top. Bake for 50 minutes, until springy to a gentle touch. Cool in the tin for 5 minutes, then transfer to a wire rack to cool. Drizzle with honey, if you like.

Pumpkin fruit cake

This is a really delicious fruit cake, and the pumpkin gives it that little extra.

1. Preheat oven to moderately slow (160°C). Grease a 20cm (base measurement) round cake tin and line the base with baking paper.
2. Use electric beaters to cream the butter, brown sugar and golden syrup until pale. Add the pumpkin, then add the eggs one at a time, beating after each addition.
3. Fold in the flour then the dried fruit and cherries. Spread into the tin, and smooth the surface. Press almonds into the top of the cake. Bake for 1 hour 30 minutes, until a skewer inserted into the centre comes out clean.
4. Cool in the tin for 10 minutes, then turn out onto a wire rack to cool.

PREP TIME: 25 MINS
COOKING TIME: 1 HOUR 30 MINS
SERVES 12

- 125g butter, at room temperature, chopped
- ¾ cup brown sugar
- 1 tbsp golden syrup, warmed
- 1 cup warm, cooked, mashed pumpkin
- 2 eggs
- 1½ cups self-raising flour
- 2 cups mixed dried fruit
- 1 cup glacé cherries
- blanched almonds, to decorate

Chocolate layer cake

PREP TIME: 30 MINS
COOKING TIME: 20–25 MINS
SERVES 8

This recipe was handed down to me from my mother and was always very popular in the family. Everyone loves chocolate cake!

1¾ cups self-raising flour
1 cup white sugar
2 tsp bicarb soda
¼ tsp salt
½ cup cocoa powder
125g soft butter, chopped
1 cup milk
1 tsp vanilla essence
2 eggs
cocoa powder, to dust

MOCK CREAM
125g unsalted butter
⅓ cup sugar

1. Preheat the oven to moderate (180°C). Grease two 20cm (base measurement) round shallow tins, and line the bases with baking paper.

2. Sift the dry ingredients into a bowl. Add the butter, milk and vanilla, and beat vigorously with a wooden spoon for 2 minutes.

3. Add the eggs and beat a further 2 minutes. Spread into the tins, and smooth the surface. Bake for 20–25 minutes, until springy to a gentle touch in the centre. Turn onto wire racks to cool.

4. To make the mock cream, use electric beaters to cream the butter and sugar until pale. Pour cold water onto the mixture, then drain off. Beat for another 2 minutes. Repeat this 5 more times, until the mixture is very light and fluffy.

5. Sandwich the cakes together with mock cream, and dust with cocoa powder.

Cinnamon nut cake

PREP TIME: 20 MINS
COOKING TIME: 30 MINS
SERVES 10

60g butter, at room temperature, chopped
½ cup white sugar
1 egg, separated
1 cup self-raising flour
pinch of salt
½ cup milk
icing sugar, to dust

WALNUT FILLING
1 cup brown sugar, firmly packed
½ cup chopped walnuts
¼ cup plain flour
20g butter, melted
½ tsp ground cinnamon

1. Preheat the oven to moderate (180°C). Grease a 20cm (base measurement) square cake tin, and line the base with baking paper, hanging over two sides. First make the filling by mixing all the ingredients together. Set aside.

2. Use electric beaters to cream the butter and sugar until white and fluffy. Add the egg yolk and beat until combined. Fold in half the sifted flour and salt, then half the milk. Repeat with remaining flour and salt, and the milk. Beat the egg white until stiff peaks form, and fold into the mixture.

3. Carefully spread half the mixture into the tin, then gently sprinkle the walnut filling over. Top with the remaining cake mixture. Bake for 30 minutes, until golden. Cool in the tin for 30 minutes, then lift out onto a wire rack to cool.

4. Cut into fingers or squares to serve, and dust with icing sugar.

Melt and mix Christmas cake

PREP TIME: 20 MINS
COOKING TIME: 2¾ HOURS
SERVES 16

1.5kg mixed dried fruit
2 tbsp sherry, rum or brandy
1 green apple, peeled and coarsely grated
1 tbsp honey or golden syrup
1 cup brown sugar
4 eggs
250g butter, melted and cooled
2 cups plain flour
1 tsp mixed spice
1 tsp salt
extra sherry, to brush
white icing, optional

This cake is great because you can double it or halve it and it still works. It is my mother's recipe and I use it all the time.

1. Place the dried fruit into a large basin. Add the sherry, apple, honey and sugar. Mix well with a large wooden spoon. Use your hands to break up any lumps of dried fruit if necessary. Leave fruit mixture to stand for 2 hours.

2. Preheat the oven to slow (140°C). Grease a 23cm (base measurement) round deep cake tin and line the base and sides with three layers of baking paper.

3. Add the eggs, butter, sifted flour, spice and salt. Stir in until evenly combined. Spoon into the prepared tin, and smooth the surface.

4. Bake for 2¾ hours, until a skewer comes out clean when inserted into the centre. Brush with the extra sherry, and cool in the tin. Decorate with white icing, if using.

NOTE: If you can, it is good to leave the fruit mixture overnight. Place it in the fridge as this will help give it flavour.

Lemon cheesecake

We had so many lemon trees in our backyard that whenever they were in season we would make lemon cheesecakes to try to use them up!

PREP TIME: 30 MINS
COOKING TIME: 35 MINS
SERVES 8

125g plain sweet biscuits, crushed
80g butter, melted

FILLING

250g cream cheese, at room temperature, chopped
395g can condensed milk
¼ cup lemon juice
2 tsp finely grated lemon rind

TOPPING

2 eggs, separated
½ cup caster sugar

1. Preheat the oven to moderate (180°C). Combine the biscuits and butter, and press into the base and halfway up the sides of a 20cm (base measurement) springform tin. Refrigerate for 20 minutes.

2. Use electric beaters to beat the cream cheese until smooth. Add the condensed milk, lemon juice, rind and egg yolks. Beat until combined. Pour into the chilled base.

3. Bake for 30 minutes, until just firm to a light touch. Cool to room temperature.

4. Preheat the oven to moderate (180°C). Use electric beaters to beat the egg whites until stiff peaks form, then gradually add half the sugar, beating well after each addition. Fold in the rest of the sugar. Spread over the filling, and bake for 5 minutes, to lightly brown the meringue.

Rainbow cake

PREP TIME: 25 MINS
COOKING TIME: 30 MINS
SERVES 8

250g butter, at room temperature, chopped
1 cup white sugar
2 tsp vanilla essence
3 eggs
3 cups plain flour
2 tsp baking powder
¾ cup milk
few drops rose pink food colouring
2 tbsp cocoa powder
½ cup raspberry or strawberry jam
tinted icing sugar, to dust

NOTE: To tint the icing sugar, place pure icing sugar into a small plastic bag and add a few drops of food colouring. Use your fingers to rub through the plastic to disperse the colouring evenly through the icing sugar. Any colouring can be used, for example pink or chocolate. Pure icing sugar should only be used for cake decorating.

This recipe is very old. My grandmother used to make it, and whenever she did there were cries of delight in our house.

1 Preheat the oven to moderate (170°C). Grease three 18cm (base measurement) round, shallow pans and line the bases with baking paper.

2 Cream the butter, sugar and vanilla in the small bowl of an electric mixer until white and fluffy. Beat in the eggs one at a time. Transfer to a larger bowl.

3 In a separate bowl, sift the flour and baking powder together. Fold in the milk and flour in batches into the cake mix, alternating between the two. Divide mixture into three equal portions. Tint one with pink food colouring, and stir the cocoa into one other to make it a chocolate mixture. Leave the remaining portion plain.

4 Spoon mixtures into separate tins, and smooth the surface. Bake for 30 minutes, or until springy to a gentle touch in the centre. Cool in the tins for 5 minutes, then turn out onto a wire rack to cool.

5 Place the chocolate layer onto a serving plate. Spread with jam, and place the pink layer onto the chocolate. Spread with jam, then place the white cake on top. Dust with tinted icing sugar.

Chocolate ripple cake

PREP TIME: 25 MINS
COOKING TIME: 40 MINS
SERVES 8

125g butter, at room temperature, chopped
¾ cup white sugar
2 eggs
1½ cups self-raising flour
½ cup milk

RIPPLE MIXTURE
10g butter, chopped
¼ cup white sugar
⅓ cup chopped walnuts
1 tbsp cocoa powder

1. Preheat the oven to moderate (180°C). Grease a 20cm (base measurement) springform tin, and line the base with baking paper.

2. Use electric beaters to cream the butter and sugar until white and fluffy. Add the eggs one at a time, beating well after each addition. Fold in half the flour, then the milk, then remaining flour. Spoon half the mixture into the tin.

3. For the ripple mixture, combine the ingredients, rubbing with your fingertips until crumbly. Sprinkle half the mixture over the cake batter in the tin. Spread remaining batter into the tin, and sprinkle with remaining ripple mixture. Bake for 40 minutes, or until cake is springy to a gentle touch.

4. Cool in the tin for 10 minutes, then release the sides and place onto a wire rack to cool.

Banana cake with caramel icing

PREP TIME: 30 MINS
COOKING TIME: 45–50 MINS
SERVES 8–10

60g butter, at room temperature
1 cup white sugar
1 tsp vanilla essence
pinch of salt
¼ cup warm milk
1 egg
3 medium bananas, well mashed
1½ cups plain flour
1 tsp bicarb soda
1 tsp baking powder

ICING
1 cup brown sugar
2 tbsp milk
1 tbsp butter
1 tsp vanilla essence

NOTE: Be careful when making the icing – if you cook it too hard it thickens too quickly and you get white spots when it cools.

This is my favourite cake. My mother always had a saying that a banana cake isn't a banana cake without caramel icing. I agree.

1. Preheat the oven to moderate (180°C). Grease a 20cm x 10cm (base measurement) loaf tin and line with baking paper, hanging over the two long sides.

2. Use electric beaters to cream the butter, sugar, vanilla and salt until white and fluffy, adding half the warm milk to help dissolve the sugar.

3. Beat in the egg then the mashed banana until evenly combined. Sift the flour, bicarb and baking powder over and fold in, then the remaining milk.

4. Spoon into the prepared tin and smooth the surface. Bake for 45–50 minutes, until springy to a gentle touch in the centre. Cover loosely with foil if it is browning too much during cooking. Stand in the tin for 10 minutes, then turn out onto a wire rack to cool.

5. To make the icing, combine the sugar, milk and butter in a small saucepan and stir over medium-low heat to dissolve the sugar. Bring to the boil, then reduce heat and simmer gently for exactly 5 minutes. Remove from the heat and stir in the vanilla. Beat with a wooden spoon until thickened slightly, then quickly spread over the top of the cake.

Orange cake

This is my own recipe and it's delicious!

1. Preheat the oven to moderately slow (160°C). Grease a 25cm (base measurement) round cake tin and line the base with baking paper.

2. Use electric beaters to cream butter and sugar until white and fluffy. Beat in the milk, sour cream, yolks and orange rind until combined. Fold in the flour.

3. Use clean beaters to beat the egg whites to soft peaks, and fold into the mixture. Spoon into the tin, and smooth the surface. Bake for about 1 hour 15 minutes, until springy to a gentle touch in the centre. Cover the top of the tin loosely with foil if it starts to become too brown before the cake is fully cooked. Leave in the tin for 5 minutes, then turn out onto a wire rack to cool.

4. To make the icing, combine the ingredients in a bowl and mix until smooth. Spread over the cooled cake.

PREP TIME: 30 MINS
COOKING TIME: 1 HOUR 15 MINS
SERVES 12

250g butter, at room temperature, chopped
2 cups white sugar
⅓ cup milk
1½ cups sour cream
3 eggs, separated
2 tbsp finely grated orange rind
4 cups self-raising flour

ORANGE ICING

2 cups icing sugar
10g butter
2-3 tbsp boiling water
1 tsp finely grated orange rind

Patty cakes

PREP TIME: 30 MINS
COOKING TIME: 15 MINS
MAKES 18

125g butter
1 cup white sugar
1 tsp vanilla essence
2 eggs
2 cups self-raising flour
¾ cup milk
⅔ cup cream, whipped
icing sugar, to dust

NOTE: If you don't have patty cake tins, use medium muffin tins.

1. Preheat the oven to moderate (180°C). Grease 18 patty cake tins, or line with paper cases.

2. Use electric beaters to cream butter, sugar and vanilla until white and fluffy. Add the eggs one at a time, beating well after each addition. Fold in half the sifted flour, half the milk, then the remaining flour and milk.

3. Spoon into patty cake tins, and bake for 15 minutes until risen and springy to a gentle touch in the centre. Leave in the tins for 2 minutes, then lift out onto a wire rack to cool.

4. To make into butterfly cakes, cut out the centre of each cake, and cut in half. Fill with whipped cream, and replace 'wings'. Dust lightly with icing sugar. Alternatively, ice the patty cakes as desired.

Speedway

PREP TIME: 10 MINS
COOKING TIME: 50 MINS
SERVES 8

125g butter, at room temperature, chopped
1 cup white sugar
2 eggs
2 cups self-raising flour
pinch of salt
¾ cup milk
1 tsp vanilla essence
icing sugar, to dust

The word 'speed' describes this recipe perfectly – all the ingredients go in and it's so easy to prepare.

1 Preheat the oven to 160°C. Grease a 20cm (base measurement) round cake tin and line the base with baking paper.

2 Use electric beaters to beat all the ingredients together for 5 minutes. Pour into prepared tin and bake for 50 minutes, until springy to a gentle touch.

3 Leave in the tin for 5 minutes, then turn out onto a wire rack to cool. Dust with icing sugar.

Pineapple fruit cake

PREP TIME: 20 MINS
COOKING TIME: 1 HOUR 45 MINS
SERVES 12

500g mixed dried fruit
440g can crushed pineapple in natural juice
1 cup white sugar
125g butter
1 tbsp mixed spice
1 tsp bicarb soda
1 cup self-raising flour
1 cup plain flour
2 eggs, lightly beaten

NOTE: Do not put icing on this cake as the pineapple against the icing will cause fermentation and spoil the cake.

This recipe has a slightly different taste from other fruit cakes. The pineapple adds something special to the mix.

1 Preheat the oven to 160°C. Grease a 20cm (base measurement) round cake tin and line the base with baking paper.

2 Place the mixed dried fruit, pineapple, sugar, butter, spice and bicarb into a large saucepan. Stir over medium heat until combined, then bring to the boil and cook for 3 minutes. Set aside to cool.

3 Sift the flours over the mixture and add the eggs. Fold together until evenly combined. Spoon into the tin and bake for 1 hour 45 minutes, or until firm to a gentle touch in the centre. Cool in the tin for 30 minutes, then turn out onto a wire rack to cool completely.

Lime and buttermilk cake

1. Preheat oven to moderate (170°C). Grease a 22cm (base measurement) round cake tin, and line the base with baking paper.

2. Use electric beaters to cream the butter, sugar and lime rind until white and fluffy. Add the egg yolks one at a time, beating well after each addition.

3. Add half the buttermilk, half the lime juice, and half the flour and fold through. Add the remaining buttermilk, lime juice and flour, and fold through. Use electric beaters to beat the egg whites to soft peaks. Fold into the cake mixture, and spoon into the tin. Smooth the surface.

4. Bake for 50 minutes, or until springy to a gentle touch in the centre. Leave in the tin for 5 minutes, then turn out onto a wire rack to cool.

5. For the icing, combine all the ingredients until smooth. Spread over the cooled cake.

PREP TIME: 30 MINS
COOKING TIME: 50 MINS
SERVES 8

250g butter, at room temperature, chopped
1 cup white sugar
finely grated rind from 2 limes
3 eggs, separated
200ml buttermilk
2 tbsp lime juice
2 cups self-raising flour

ICING
1 cup icing sugar
1½ tbsp lime juice
1 tsp water

Walnut cake

PREP TIME: 40 MINS
COOKING TIME: 20 MINS
SERVES 8

60g butter, at room temperature, chopped
1 cup white sugar
3 eggs
1½ cups self-raising flour
3 tsp cocoa powder
1 tsp mixed spice
¾ cup milk
½ cup chopped walnuts, plus extra, to decorate
300ml cream, whipped
walnut pieces, to decorate
grated chocolate, optional

CHOCOLATE BUTTER ICING

80g butter, at room temperature, chopped
1 tsp vanilla essence
1 cup icing sugar mixture
1 tbs cocoa powder
2 tsp milk

1 Preheat oven to moderate (180°C). Grease two 20cm (base measurement) round shallow tins and line the bases with baking paper.

2 Use electric beaters to cream the butter and sugar until pale. Add the eggs one at a time, beating well after each addition.

3 Sift the flour, cocoa and mixed spice together and fold into the butter mixture, along with the milk. Stir in the nuts. Spread into the cake tins, and smooth the surface. Bake for 20 minutes, until springy to a gentle touch in the centre. Stand in tins for 5 minutes, then turn out onto a wire rack to cool.

4 To make the icing, use electric beaters to beat the butter and vanilla until very soft, then add the icing sugar then cocoa and milk a little at a time, beating constantly, until fluffy. Spread onto one cake, and decorate with extra walnuts, and grated chocolate if you like.

5 Spread whipped cream onto the un-iced cake, and top with the iced cake.

Baked cheesecake

PREP TIME: 30 MINS
+ 3 HOURS CHILLING
COOKING TIME: 45 MINS
SERVES 8

250g Butternut Snap biscuits, crushed
1 tsp mixed spice
100g butter, melted

FILLING
500g cream cheese, at room temperature, chopped
$2/3$ cup white sugar
1 tsp vanilla essence
1 tsp lemon juice
4 eggs

NOTE: Serve this with cream and berries, if you like.

1. Preheat the oven to moderate (180°C) and grease a 20cm (base measurement) springform tin. Combine biscuits, mixed spice and butter, and press into the base of the tin. Refrigerate for 20 minutes.

2. Use electric beaters to beat the cream cheese, sugar, vanilla and lemon juice until smooth and creamy. Add the eggs one at a time, beating well after each addition. Pour onto the chilled base.

3. Stand tin on a baking tray, and bake for 45 minutes, until just set. Cool to room temperature, then chill for 3 hours, until firm.

Plain buttercake

PREP TIME: 30 MINS
COOKING TIME: 55–60 MINS
SERVES 8

125g butter, at room temperature, chopped
¾ cup white sugar
½ cup milk
1 tsp vanilla essence
1 cup plain flour
½ cup cornflour
1 tsp baking powder
pinch of salt
4 egg whites

ICING
1 cup icing sugar
10g butter
1½ tbsp boiling water

This is the base of the recipe for the Peach Blossom cake, without the pink colouring. This is a good one to start on before moving to the Peach Blossom if you're a bit nervous!

1 Preheat the oven to moderately slow (160°C). Grease an 18cm (base measurement) round cake tin and line the base with baking paper.

2 Cream the butter and sugar in the small bowl of an electric mixer until white and fluffy. Gradually add half the milk to help dissolve the sugar, and beat well. Beat in the vanilla. Transfer to a larger bowl.

3 Sift the flour, cornflour, baking powder and salt together 3 times. Fold into the butter mixture, then add the remaining milk (don't worry if the mixture appears curdled at this stage). In another bowl, use clean beaters to beat the egg whites to stiff peaks. Fold half the egg whites into the cake batter, then fold in the remaining egg whites.

4 Transfer to the tin, and smooth the surface. Bake for 55–60 minutes, until the cake is springy to a gentle touch in the centre and comes away from the sides of the tin. Turn out onto a clean tea towel covered with a sheet of baking paper. Leave to cool.

5 To make the icing, combine the ingredients until smooth. Spread over the top of the cooled cake, and leave to set.

Small cakes

1. Preheat the oven to moderately hot (200°C). Grease 24 patty cake tins, or line with paper cases.

2. Use electric beaters to cream butter, sugar and vanilla until white and fluffy. Add the eggs one at a time, beating well after each addition. Fold in half the sifted flour, half the milk, then the remaining flour and milk.

3. Spoon into patty pans, and bake for 10–15 minutes until risen and springy to a gentle touch in the centre. Leave in the tins for 2 minutes, then lift out onto a wire rack to cool.

4. To make the buttercream icing, use electric beaters to beat the butter and vanilla until very soft, then add the icing sugar a little at a time, beating constantly, until white and fluffy. Spread onto the cakes, and top with a flower if using.

PREP TIME: 30 MINS
COOKING TIME: 10–15 MINS
MAKES 24

100g butter, at room temperature, chopped
½ cup white sugar
1 tsp vanilla essence
2 eggs
1 cup self-raising flour
2 tbsp milk

BUTTERCREAM ICING

125g butter, at room temperature, chopped
1 tsp vanilla essence
1½ cups icing sugar mixture
little icing flowers, to decorate, optional

NOTE: If you don't have patty cake tins, use mini muffin tins – or make them slightly larger in medium muffin tins.

Carrot cake

PREP TIME: 30 MINS
COOKING TIME: 45 MINS
SERVES 8

2 eggs
1 cup white sugar
¾ cup vegetable oil
1 tsp vanilla essence
1 cup plain flour
1 tsp bicarb soda
½ tsp mixed spice
pinch of salt
1½ cups finely grated carrot
½ cup chopped walnuts

ICING

60g cream cheese, at room temperature, chopped
30g butter, at room temperature, chopped
1 tsp finely grated lemon rind
1½ cups sifted icing sugar

1. Preheat the oven to moderate (170°C). Grease a 20cm (base measurement) round cake tin and line the base with baking paper.

2. Use electric beaters to beat the eggs, sugar, oil and vanilla until combined. Add the sifted dry ingredients and beat on low speed until combined. Stir in the carrot and walnuts.

3. Spoon into the tin. Bake for 45 minutes, until springy to a gentle touch in the centre. Stand in the tin for 10 minutes, then turn out onto a wire rack to cool completely.

4. For the icing, use electric beaters to beat the cream cheese, butter and lemon rind until creamy. Add the icing sugar a little at a time, beating constantly. Spread over the top of the cooled cake.

Biscuit cake

PREP TIME: 30 MINS
COOKING TIME: 15–20 MINS PER BATCH
SERVES 8

250g butter, at room temperature, chopped
1 cup white sugar
1 tsp vanilla essence
2 eggs
4 cups plain flour
1 tsp baking powder
pinch of salt
¼ cup milk
½ cup raspberry jam

ICING
2½ cups icing sugar mixture
10g soft butter
3 tbsp boiling water

NOTE: Dough scraps can be cut into pieces and cooked to make small biscuits.

This is a bit different from other cakes and keeps very well — if you can stop your family from eating it immediately, that is!

1. Preheat oven to 170°C. Line 3 large oven trays with baking paper.

2. Use electric beaters to cream the butter, sugar and vanilla until white and fluffy. Add the eggs one at a time, beating well after each addition.

3. Sift the flour, baking powder and salt together, and add in batches, alternating with the milk. Mix to a firm dough.

4. Turn out onto a lightly floured surface and use a rolling pin to roll out to 5mm thick. Using a plate as a guide, cut out five 18cm rounds from the dough. Place onto trays (you will have to cook these in batches) and cook for 15–20 minutes, until golden brown.

5. Cool on the trays for 5 minutes, then transfer to a wire rack to cool completely. When cool, spread four of the biscuits with jam and sandwich together, stacking to make a five-layer 'cake'.

6. For the icing, combine all the ingredients until smooth. Spread over top and sides of the cake.

Donna Latter's chocolate cake

PREP TIME: 20 MINS
COOKING TIME: 1 HOUR
SERVES 8

1¾ cups self-raising flour
1¼ cups white sugar
2 tbsp cocoa powder
½ tsp bicarb soda
125g butter, at room temperature, chopped
2 eggs
1 cup milk

ICING
200g dark chocolate
60g butter

NOTE: This icing is quite rich, great for special occasions. If you want something a little less fancy, use a regular chocolate icing.

This was a prize that was awarded in the memory of Donna Latter by her family, and to win the inaugural cup was the biggest thrill of my cooking life. I took home the cup (the first I had ever won), and a $50 prize at the state final of the CWA *Land* Cooking Contest.

1. Preheat the oven to 180°C. Grease a 20cm (base measurement) round cake tin and line the base with baking paper.

2. Combine all the ingredients in a large mixing bowl, and using electric beaters beat for about 3 minutes, until combined, smooth, and the mixture is thick and pale. Pour into the tin and smooth the surface.

3. Bake for about 1 hour, until a skewer comes out clean when inserted, and cake comes away from the sides of the tin. Cool in the tin for 5 minutes, then turn out onto a wire rack to cool completely.

4. For the icing, melt the chocolate and butter together in a saucepan over low heat. Cool for 15 minutes, then spread onto the cooled cake.

Sponges

Lots of people won't attempt sponges – they see them as tricky. To make a sponge, the first step is to beat your eggs until they are fluffy and light. I beat the egg whites with sugar first and then add the yolk. Don't overbeat them, or the sponge will be tough. I use an electric beater now, but when I started it was a hand egg-beater. When my hand got tired, my husband Clyde would take over. ❁ I always strain my jam for the filling so there are no seeds, and smear on just enough jam to hold the two sponge layers together.

Never-fail sponge

PREP TIME: 30 MINS
COOKING TIME: 20 MINS
SERVES 8

3 eggs, separated
1 cup caster sugar
½ cup cold water
1 tsp vanilla essence
2 tsp baking powder
1 cup plain flour
1 tbsp cornflour
jam and whipped cream to fill
icing sugar, to dust

TIP: If you like, sprinkle sandwich tins lightly with very fine breadcrumbs before baking. To decorate the sponge, you can lay a doily on top before dusting with icing sugar. Carefully remove to reveal the pattern.

This never-fail sponge only ever failed for me twice — pretty good odds for all the years!

1 Preheat the oven to moderate (180°C). Grease two 20cm (base measurement) round shallow tins and line the bases with baking paper.

2 Use electric beaters to beat the egg yolks, sugar, water and vanilla for 10 minutes, until very thick and pale. Use clean beaters to beat the egg whites and baking powder until stiff peaks form.

3 Fold the sifted flours into the yolk mixture, then the egg whites. Divide evenly between the tins, and bake for 20 minutes, until springy to a gentle touch in the centre. Lay newspaper then a clean tea towel onto a wire rack, and turn the cakes out onto it. Leave to cool.

4 Spread one sponge generously with your favourite jam, and then whipped cream. Place the other sponge on top.

Sponge lilies

PREP TIME: 15 MINS
COOKING TIME: 5 MINS PER BATCH
MAKES ABOUT 25

2 eggs, separated
¼ cup white sugar
½ cup self-raising flour
pinch of salt
1 tbsp hot water
1 cup cream, whipped
icing sugar, to dust

NOTE: You will probably have to cook in batches. Gently stir the batter until smooth before spooning out the second batch. Another way to create the folded sponges so they hold their shape (and don't get little holes in them from toothpicks) is to fold them gently while hot, then put them into an empty egg carton to cool. They can also be folded into a triangular shape if you prefer.

1. Preheat the oven to moderate (180°C) and line 2 large baking trays with baking paper.

2. Using electric beaters, beat the egg whites until soft peaks form. Gradually beat in the sugar, then beat in the egg yolks.

3. Fold in the flour and salt, then the water. Drop level tablespoons of mixture onto the tray, and use the back of a spoon to spread to 6cm rounds. Cook for 5 minutes, until just lightly golden.

4. Working one at a time, lift the sponges from the tray with a spatula, and gently fold over so the sides just touch. Use a toothpick to hold in place, and transfer to a wire rack to cool.

5. Spoon whipped cream into the sponges, and dust with icing sugar.

Chocolate sponge

PREP TIME: 30 MINS
COOKING TIME: 20 MINS
SERVES 8

Winning the award for this cake was something that has eluded me over the years — until the Sydney Royal Easter Show in 2011! It's a little tricky to make as too little cocoa means not enough colour; too much cocoa and it goes flat.

1 cup plain flour (less 1 tbsp)
1 tsp baking powder
2 tbsp cocoa powder
4 eggs, separated
pinch of salt
1 cup caster sugar
1 tsp vanilla essence
30g butter, melted
2 tbsp boiling water
icing sugar, to dust

MOCK CREAM

125g unsalted butter
½ cup caster sugar
1 tsp vanilla essence

NOTE: The newspaper and tea towel on the rack prevent marks from the wire rack on top of the cake.

1 Preheat the oven to moderate (180°C). Grease two 20cm (base measurement) round shallow tins and line the bases with baking paper. Sift the combined flour, baking powder and cocoa powder three times.

2 Use electric beaters to beat the egg whites and salt to soft peaks. Add the sugar gradually, beating until dissolved between each addition, until very white and glossy – this will take about 8 minutes.

3 Add the yolks and vanilla and beat briefly until just combined. Gently fold in the flour mixture, then the butter and boiling water. Divide equally between the cake tins (weigh to make sure they are the same).

4 Place cakes onto middle shelf in oven, and bake for 20 minutes, until springy to a gentle touch in the centre. Lay newspaper then a clean tea towel onto a wire rack, and turn the cakes out onto it. Leave to cool.

5 To make the mock cream, use electric beaters to cream the butter, sugar and vanilla until pale. Pour cold water onto the mixture, then drain off. Beat for another 2 minutes. Repeat this 5 more times, until the mixture is very light and fluffy.

6 Spread filling onto one cake, and top with the other. Dust with icing sugar.

Sponge roll

1. Preheat oven to moderate (180°C). Grease a Swiss roll tin (30cm x 25cm x 2cm deep – see note) and line the base with baking paper, hanging over the two long sides of the tin. Sift the combined flours and baking powder three times.

2. Using electric beaters, beat the egg whites and salt until soft peaks form, then gradually add the sugar, beating constantly until stiff peaks form. Add the egg yolks and vanilla, and beat until combined.

3. Gently fold in the flour mixture, and spread evenly into the tin. Bake for 15 minutes, until springy to a gentle touch in the centre.

4. Meanwhile, lay out another sheet of baking paper, and sprinkle generously with extra sugar. Turn the sponge out and place on a tea towel. Spread quickly with jam and then roll up, starting at the short end. Leave to cool for around 15-20 minutes. Then slice and serve.

PREP TIME: 20 MINS
COOKING TIME: 15 MINS + 20 MINS COOLING
SERVES 8

⅔ cup cornflour
1 slightly rounded tbsp plain flour
1 tsp baking powder
3 eggs, separated
pinch of salt
½ cup white sugar
1 tsp vanilla essence
2 tbsp white sugar, extra
⅓ cup strawberry jam

NOTE: These tins vary slightly between brands, but are all pretty similar.

Sponge powder puffs

PREP TIME: 20 MINS
COOKING TIME: 8–9 MINS PER BATCH
MAKES ABOUT 25 (FILLED)

3 eggs, separated
¾ cup white sugar
1 tsp vanilla essence
10g soft butter
1 tbsp warm water
1 cup self-raising flour
pinch of salt
icing sugar to dust

FILLING
125g soft butter
½ cup white sugar
2 tbsp milk
1 tsp vanilla essence

NOTE: You will have to cook in batches. Gently stir the batter until smooth before spooning out the second batch.

I make my sponge powder puffs on a scone tray. They are beautiful to eat — when you take a bite they just melt away in your mouth.

1 Preheat the oven to moderate (180°C). Line 2 large baking trays with baking paper.

2 Using electric beaters, beat the egg whites until soft peaks form. Gradually beat in the sugar, then vanilla, then the egg yolks.

3 Combine the butter and warm water to melt the butter. Fold the sifted flour and salt into the egg mixture, then the butter and water.

4 Drop heaped teaspoonfuls of mixture onto the tray, leaving room for spreading. Cook for 8–9 minutes, until lightly golden. Transfer to a wire rack to cool.

5 For the filling, use electric beaters to cream the butter and sugar until white and fluffy. Beat in the milk and vanilla. Spread onto half the sponges, and sandwich with the others. Dust with icing sugar.

Cinnamon sponge

PREP TIME: 20 MINS
COOKING TIME: 20 MINS
SERVES 8

1 cup plain flour
2 tsp ground cinnamon
1 tsp baking powder
pinch of salt
4 eggs
¾ cup sugar
1 tsp vanilla essence
¼ cup boiling water
1 tsp butter
2 tsp golden syrup

FILLING
300ml cream
1 tsp vanilla essence

TOPPING
2 tsp caster sugar
¼ tsp ground cinnamon

NOTE: The newspaper and tea towel on the rack prevent marks from the wire rack on the top of the cake.

This is one of my family's favourite sponges, as they love the cinnamon flavour.

1. Preheat the oven to moderate (180°C). Grease two 20cm (base measurement) round, shallow cake tins and line the bases with baking paper. Sift the combined flour, cinnamon, baking powder and salt three times.

2. Use electric beaters to beat the eggs, sugar and vanilla for 10 minutes, until pale, frothy and increased in volume. Gently fold in the flour mixture, then the combined water, butter and golden syrup. Divide equally between the cake tins (weigh to make sure they are the same).

3. Bake for 20 minutes, until springy to a gentle touch in the centre. Lay newspaper then a clean tea towel onto a wire rack, and turn the cakes out onto it. Leave to cool.

4. For the filling, use electric beaters to beat the cream and vanilla to soft peaks. Spread over one cake, and top with the other. For the topping, put the caster sugar and cinnamon into a small sieve and dust over the cake.

Honey sponge roll

PREP TIME: 30 MINS
COOKING TIME: 12–15 MINS
SERVES 8

½ cup cornflour
1 tsp plain flour
1 tsp baking powder
1 tsp mixed spice
3 eggs
½ cup caster sugar, plus extra to sprinkle
pinch of salt
1 tsp honey, warmed so it is more liquid

HONEY MOCK CREAM
125g unsalted butter
⅓ cup caster sugar
1 tbsp honey

NOTE: These tins vary slightly between brands, but are all pretty similar.

Duck eggs make a beautiful sponge. Use one duck egg to two hen's eggs.

1 Preheat the oven to moderate (180°C). Grease a Swiss roll tin (30cm x 25cm x 2cm deep – see note) and line the base with baking paper, hanging over the two long sides of the tin. Sift the combined flours, baking powder and mixed spice three times.

2 Using electric beaters, beat the eggs, sugar and salt for 10 minutes, until pale, frothy and increased in volume. Gently fold in the flour mixture, then the honey. Spread into the tin and bake for 12–15 minutes until springy to a gentle touch in the centre.

3 Meanwhile, lay out another sheet of baking paper, and sprinkle generously with caster sugar. Turn the sponge out onto the sugared paper, and starting at a short end, roll up. Leave for 20 minutes, to cool.

4 To make the mock cream, use electric beaters to cream the butter, sugar and honey until pale. Pour cold water onto the mixture, then drain off. Beat for another 2 minutes. Repeat this 5 more times, until the mixture is very light and fluffy.

5 Unroll the sponge and spread with honey mock cream. Re-roll, and slice to serve.

Puddings and desserts

When I was a girl, pudding was part of the main meal every day. When I had a young family, I made pudding every day as well. We used to have this Yearly and Meal Calendar, which showed a first course and a pudding recipe for each day of the year. I would sometimes refer to it for suggestions for what to have that day. My six grandkids love my golden syrup dumplings. They always want them when they come to visit. The recipe I use is my grandmother's recipe.

Clyde's pudding

PREP TIME: 25 MINS
COOKING TIME: 2½ HOURS
SERVES 6-8

1 cup flour
2 tbsp white sugar
pinch nutmeg
pinch of salt
250g sultanas
1 tsp bicarb soda
1 tbsp butter
1 tbsp vinegar
1 cup milk
custard to serve

My mother always used to spoil my husband Clyde, as whenever we went over to her house she cooked this pudding for him. We named it after him as a result.

1. Grease a 5-cup capacity pudding basin, and line the base with a small round of baking paper.

2. Combine the flour, sugar, nutmeg, salt and sultanas in a mixing bowl and make a well in the centre.

3. Put the bicarb into a jug, and add the butter and vinegar. Heat the milk to boiling point, and add to the jug. Pour into the dry ingredients, and stir to combine (it will be a thin batter).

4. Spoon the mixture into the pudding basin. Lay out a sheet of foil and top with a sheet of baking paper. Fold a pleat down the centre, about 4cm wide. Place paper-side-down over the top of the pudding basin. Press down around the edge and tie kitchen string around to secure (wet the string to make it easier to work with).

5. Place a trivet into a large stock pot, and sit the pudding basin on it. Pour in enough boiling water to come about two thirds of the way up the side of the basin. Cover and return water to the boil, then cook for 2½ hours. Check and top up with boiling water during cooking as necessary.

6. Carefully lift the basin from the pot, remove string and covering. Turn out onto a plate, and cut into wedges to serve, with custard.

Butterscotch rice pudding

PREP TIME: 25 MINS
COOKING TIME: 2 HOURS 10 MINS
SERVES 8

1 cup medium-grain rice
pinch of salt
4 cups milk
60g butter
½ cup brown sugar
1 tbsp milk, extra
2 eggs, separated
½ tsp vanilla essence
½ cup brown sugar, extra
ground cinnamon, to dust

1. Preheat the oven to slow (150°C). Put the rice into a sieve and wash under cold running water, then drain. Place into a 6-cup capacity ovenproof dish and stir in the salt and milk. Cover with a lid or foil, and bake for 2 hours, until the rice is cooked and has absorbed most of the milk. Remove from the oven and uncover, being careful to avoid the steam.

2. Cook the butter and brown sugar in a small saucepan, stirring until they form a syrup. Stir in the extra milk, then stir mixture into the cooked rice. Beat the egg yolks and vanilla together, stir in a spoonful of the rice mixture, then add to the dish and stir through.

3. Use electric beaters to beat the egg whites to soft peaks, then gradually add the extra brown sugar, beating to stiff peaks. Pile on top of the rice, and sprinkle lightly with cinnamon. Return to the oven for 10 minutes, until the meringue is browned.

Steamed fruit pudding

PREP TIME: 30 MINS
COOKING TIME: 2 HOURS
SERVES 8

1 cup mixed dried fruit
1 cup milk
½ cup white sugar
2 tbsp butter
1 tsp bicarb soda
1 cup self-raising flour

This is very nice served with custard, cream or ice-cream. Be warned, though — on go the kilos again!

1 Grease a 5-cup capacity pudding basin, and line the base with a small round of baking paper.

2 Combine the dried fruit, milk, sugar and butter in a saucepan and bring to the boil. Stir in the bicarb and remove from the heat. Fold in the flour.

3 Spoon the mixture into the pudding basin. Lay out a sheet of foil and top with a sheet of baking paper. Fold a pleat down the centre, about 4cm wide. Place paper-side-down over the top of the pudding basin. Press down around the edge and tie kitchen string around to secure (wet the string to make it easier to work with).

4 Place a trivet into a large stock pot, and sit the pudding basin on it. Pour in enough boiling water to come about two thirds of the way up the side of the basin. Cover and return the water to the boil, then cook for 2 hours. Check and top up with boiling water during cooking as necessary.

5 Carefully lift the basin from the pot, remove string and covering. Turn out onto a plate, and cut into wedges to serve.

Orange pudding

1. Grease a 5-cup capacity pudding basin, and line the base with a small round of baking paper.

2. Using electric beaters, cream the butter and sugar until pale and fluffy. Add the egg and beat well, then beat in the orange rind. Sift the flour and salt onto the mixture, and add the orange juice. Fold together until combined.

3. Spoon the mixture into the pudding basin. Lay out a sheet of foil and top with a sheet of baking paper. Fold a pleat down the centre, about 4cm wide. Place paper-side-down over the top of the pudding basin. Press down around the edge and tie kitchen string around to secure (wet the string to make it easier to work with).

4. Place a trivet into a large stock pot, and sit the pudding basin on it. Pour in enough boiling water to come about two thirds of the way up the side of the basin. Cover and return water to the boil, then cook for 1½ hours. Check and top up with boiling water during cooking as necessary.

5. Carefully lift the basin from the pot, remove string and covering. Turn out onto a plate. Cut into wedges and serve with the sauce.

6. For the sauce, mix the sugar and cornflour in a small saucepan. Gradually add the hot water, stirring until smooth. Add the rind, juice and butter. Stir until the butter melts and the mixture comes to the boil and thickens.

PREP TIME: 30 MINS
COOKING TIME: 1½ HOURS
SERVES 8

90g butter, at room temperature, chopped
⅓ cup white sugar
1 egg
2 tsp finely grated orange rind
1½ cups self-raising flour
pinch of salt
½ cup strained orange juice

ORANGE SAUCE

½ cup white sugar
2 tbsp cornflour
1 cup hot water
finely grated rind 1 orange
¼ cup orange juice
1 tbsp butter

Butterscotch 'sponge' pudding

PREP TIME: 15 MINS
SETTING TIME: 2 HOURS
SERVES 4–6

80g butter
1 cup brown sugar
3 eggs, separated
1 cup milk
¼ cup water
3 tsp gelatine powder
fruit and ice-cream, to serve

1. Melt the butter and sugar together in a saucepan, then transfer to a mixing bowl and set aside to cool slightly. Whisk in the egg yolks, then gradually add the milk, whisking constantly (but not too vigorously).

2. Put the water into a small bowl, and sprinkle the gelatine over. Stand for a minute to soften, then either microwave for 30 seconds, or stand the bowl in a pan of hot water, whisking with a fork until the gelatine has dissolved and the mixture is clear. Cool slightly, then stir into the milk mixture.

3. Refrigerate for about 10 minutes, stirring occasionally, until thickened slightly (take care not to leave it too long or it will become too set).

4. Use electric beaters to beat the egg whites to soft peaks. Fold into the milk mixture, and pour into a 6-cup capacity serving dish. Refrigerate for 2 hours, until set.

5. Spoon into bowls, and serve with fresh fruit and ice-cream.

Monday's pudding

This is a recipe from my grandma's recipe book. Monday was washing day, which would take all day, so Monday's pudding was therefore always a plain one — though still delicious!

PREP TIME: 20 MINS
COOKING TIME: 1½ HOURS
SERVES 6

40g butter, at room temperature
½ cup white sugar
1 tsp vanilla essence
1 egg
1½ cups self-raising flour
½ cup milk
drizzle of golden syrup, optional
custard, to serve

1 Grease a 6-cup capacity pudding basin, and line the base with a small round of baking paper.

2 Use electric beaters to cream the butter, sugar, vanilla and egg.

3 Fold in the flour and milk. Spoon into the pudding basin. Lay out a sheet of foil and top with a sheet of baking paper. Fold a pleat down the centre, about 4cm wide. Place paper-side-down over the base, fold down over the edge and tie kitchen string around to secure (wet the string to make it easier to work with).

4 Place a trivet into a large stock pot, and sit the pudding basin on it. Pour in enough boiling water to come about two thirds the way up the side of the basin. Cover and return water to the boil, then cook for 1½ hours. Check and top up with boiling water during cooking as necessary.

5 Carefully lift the basin from the pot, remove string and covering. Turn out onto a plate, and cut into wedges to serve, with a drizzle of golden syrup if you like, and custard.

Apple pie

PREP TIME: 30 MINS
COOKING TIME: ABOUT 40 MINS
SERVES 8

FILLING

6 Granny Smith apples
1 tbsp water
¾ cup white sugar

PASTRY

1¾ cups cup plain flour
1 tsp baking powder
pinch of salt
2 tsp white sugar, extra
125g butter, chopped
3 tbsp water, approximately, extra

1. Preheat the oven to moderate (170°C). Peel, quarter and core the apples, then cut each quarter into 3 slices. Place into a large saucepan with 1 tbsp water. Cover and cook over medium heat for about 3 minutes, until just tender. Mix in the sugar, and leave to cool.

2. To make the pastry, sift the flour, baking powder, salt and extra sugar into a mixing bowl. Use your fingertips to rub in the butter until the mixture resembles breadcrumbs. Add the water, mixing in with a butter knife until evenly moistened. Add a little more water if necessary.

3. Gather the dough together and turn onto a lightly floured surface. Divide into 2 portions. Roll out one portion and use to line the base of a 20cm (base measurement) pie dish. Roll out the remaining pastry to fit the top of the dish.

4. Drain the apples, and spoon into the pastry-lined dish. Place the top pastry over and press the edges to seal. Trim off any excess pastry around the sides, and prick a few holes in the top. Bake for 35–40 minutes, until golden brown.

Pavlova

This is such a popular Aussie dessert. Adapt to your own taste by adding whatever fruit you like: passionfruit, kiwi fruit, raspberries, strawberries, blueberries — whatever is in season.

PREP TIME: 20 MINS
COOKING TIME: 1½ HOURS
SERVES 10

6 egg whites
1½ cups caster sugar
1½ tsp white vinegar
1 tbsp cornflour
whipped cream and passionfruit, to serve

1. Preheat the oven to very slow (120°C). Grease a baking tray and line with a sheet of baking paper.

2. Use electric beaters to beat the egg whites until stiff peaks form. Add sugar a tablespoon at a time, beating until the sugar has dissolved between each addition.

3. Keep adding and beating until the mixture is thick, white and glossy. Beat in the vinegar and cornflour. Use a large spoon to transfer to the tray, then shape into a 22cm round.

4. Bake for 1½ hours, then turn off the oven, prop the door open slightly and leave to cool completely.

5. When cool, top with whipped cream and passionfruit.

Rich Christmas pudding

Boil it in a cloth and serve it at Christmas time with brandy — it's yummy!

PREP TIME: 30 MINS
COOKING TIME: 4½ HOURS
SERVES 16–20 (2 PUDDINGS)

250g suet (or butter), finely chopped
pinch of salt
500g brown sugar
500g sultanas
500g raisins
500g currants
125g mixed peel
8 eggs, lightly beaten
60g chopped blanched almonds
1 tbsp brandy
500g plain flour
1 tsp mixed spice
1½ cups fresh breadcrumbs
1 tsp bicarb soda
1 tbsp milk
4 lemons, halved
brandy custard, to serve

1. Rub the suet (or butter), salt and sugar together in a very large basin. Mix in the fruit, peel and eggs. Add the almonds, brandy, sifted flour and spice, and breadcrumbs. Dissolve the bicarb in the milk, and mix in.

2. Fill 2 large stockpots three quarters full with water, and bring to the boil. Add the juice of two lemons to each pot, then throw in the squeezed lemons. Place 2 pudding cloths or 50cm square pieces of calico (see note) into a pot, and boil for 1 minute, to heat through.

3. Remove the cloths from the pot, cool slightly, then wring out. Drape one into a colander. Spoon half the pudding mixture into the cloth. Gather up firmly around the mixture, allowing about 2cm of room for the pudding to swell during cooking. Tie securely with kitchen string. Repeat with the other cloth and remaining mixture.

4. Place a saucer into the base of each pot. Lower the puddings into the boiling water, and boil, covered, for 4½ hours. Check and top up with boiling water as needed – the pudding must remain submerged at all times. Turn slightly (not over) every 45 minutes so it cooks evenly.

5. Remove from the water, and allow to drain well. Untie string and gently peel back the cloth and serve with brandy custard.

TIPS
- Halve the recipe if you only want one pudding.
- To get a nice shape, you can suspend the pudding from a large wooden spoon placed across the pot. In this case, cover the pan with a double thickness of foil and tightly cover.
- This pudding can be made 7–10 days before use and reheated, or eaten cold if butter is used instead of suet.

NOTE: To prepare a new pudding cloth or calico for use, soak overnight in cold water, then boil for 20 minutes, and rinse well.

Lemon meringue pie

PREP TIME: 35 MINS
COOKING TIME: 40 MINS
SERVES 6

PASTRY

1½ cups plain flour
125g cold butter, chopped
3 tbsp chilled water, approximately

FILLING

2 tbsp plain flour
2 tbsp cornflour
½ cup white sugar
½ cup lemon juice
1 cup boiling water
2 egg yolks
1 tbsp butter
finely grated rind 1 lemon

MERINGUE

2 egg whites
⅓ cup caster sugar

1. To make the pastry, put the flour into a bowl and add the butter. Use your fingertips to rub in until the mixture resembles breadcrumbs. Add almost all the water, and use a knife to cut into the flour mixture until it begins to clump together. Pinch a bit with your fingers to check if it is moist enough – if not, add a little bit more water.

2. Gather the dough together and turn out onto a lightly floured surface. Roll out to fit a 23cm pie dish. Line the dish with pastry, and chill for 20 minutes. Preheat the oven to moderate (180°C). Line the pastry with a piece of baking paper, and fill with dried beans or rice. Bake for 15 minutes, then take out the paper and beans and cook a further 15 minutes, until dry and lightly golden. Cool completely.

3. For the filling, mix the flour, cornflour, sugar and lemon juice in a saucepan until smooth. Add the boiling water and cook, stirring, over medium heat, until thickened. Stir in the egg yolks, butter and lemon rind. Spoon into the pastry case, and smooth the surface. Leave to cool.

4. Preheat the oven to moderately hot (200°C). To make the meringue, use electric beaters to beat the egg whites until stiff peaks form. Add the sugar gradually, beating constantly. Spoon over the filling, swirling to make peaks. Place into the oven for 5 minutes, or until lightly browned.

Peach crumble

PREP TIME: 20 MINS
COOKING TIME: 15–20 MINS
SERVES 4-6

4 medium peaches
1 cup plain flour
60g soft butter
½ cup brown sugar

NOTE: Use canned peaches if fresh are not in season.

Try this with other fruits too — apricots, apple or even blackberries if you can find them. It is a wonderfully versatile dessert.

1 Preheat the oven to moderately slow (160°C). Score a small cross at the base of each peach, and place into a heatproof bowl. Cover with boiling water and stand for 2 minutes. Drain and cool. Slip off the skins.

2 Slice the peaches, and arrange into the base of a 4–5 cup capacity ovenproof dish.

3 Use your fingertips to rub together the flour, butter and sugar until evenly combined. Spread evenly over the peaches. Bake for 15–20 minutes, until golden.

Lemon delicious

1. Preheat the oven to moderate (170°C). Grease a 6-cup capacity ovenproof dish.

2. Beat the egg yolks with the sugar until thick and creamy, then beat in the butter, milk, flour, juice and rind.

3. Using clean beaters, beat the egg whites until soft peaks form. Add the extra sugar a little at a time, beating constantly until thick and glossy. Fold into the lemon mixture.

4. Spoon into the dish, and stand in a large baking dish. Pour in enough cold water to come halfway up the side of the dish. Bake for 50–60 minutes, until risen and golden brown. Dust lightly with icing sugar, and serve immediately.

PREP TIME: 20 MINS
COOKING TIME: 50–60 MINS
SERVES 4-6

3 eggs, separated
½ cup white sugar
30g butter, melted
1 cup milk
½ cup self-raising flour
⅓ cup lemon juice
1 tsp finely grated lemon rind
½ cup white sugar, extra
icing sugar to dust

Caramel and banana pancakes

PREP TIME: 15 MINS
COOKING TIME: 20 MINS
SERVES 4 (MAKES 8)

This is very popular with the young people in my family. My daughter Marianne serves this with ice-cream and caramel sauce.

PANCAKES
1 cup self-raising flour
pinch of salt
1 egg
1½ cups milk

TOPPING
60g butter
1 cup brown sugar
½ cup cream
4 ripe bananas, sliced

1. To make the pancakes, sift the flour and salt into a bowl and make a well in the centre. Whisk the egg and milk together and stir into the dry ingredients to make a smooth batter.

2. Preheat a large heavy-based frying pan over medium heat, and lightly grease. Pour ¼ cup of the batter into the frying pan and swirl the pan to make a thin pancake. Cook over medium heat for 1½ minutes, until golden underneath. Turn over and cook 1 more minute. Keep warm in a low oven while you cook the rest of the pancakes.

3. To make the topping, melt the butter in a frying pan, then stir in the sugar until it dissolves. Stir in the cream, add the bananas and simmer for 1 minute, until tender. Serve over the pancakes.

Golden syrup dumplings

PREP TIME: 20 MINS
COOKING TIME: 20 MINS
SERVES 4

SAUCE
2 cups water
½ cup golden syrup
½ cup brown sugar
30g butter

DUMPLINGS
20g butter
1 cup self-raising flour
⅓ cup milk

NOTE: My family love sultanas so I add a good handful before the milk.

Whenever the grandkids come home they want Gran to make them dumplings! And I always do.

1. Combine the sauce ingredients in a large saucepan, and bring to a simmer for about five minutes as this will help the sauce to thicken before adding the dumplings.

2. For the dumplings, use your fingertips to rub the butter into the flour and make a well in the centre. Add milk and stir with a wooden spoon then gather together to make a soft dough.

3. Take level tablespoons of dough and shape roughly into 12 balls. Drop gently into the simmering sauce. Cover and cook for 20 minutes.

Apple strudel

PREP TIME: 30 MINS + 1 HOUR RESTING
COOKING TIME: 35 MINS
SERVES 8

1½ cups self-raising flour
1 tbsp lard, softened
2 tsp peanut oil
¾ cup warm water
3–4 Granny Smith apples (depending on size)
2 tbsp sultanas
2 tbsp white sugar + extra to sprinkle
½ tsp ground cinnamon
40g butter, melted
cinnamon sugar, to dust
custard or ice-cream, to serve

My niece Mavis always makes this. Whenever we go to her place we put in our request for this one!

1. Place the flour into a mixing bowl and make a well in the centre. Add the lard, peanut oil and warm water. Gather the dough together and knead lightly until smooth. Wrap in plastic wrap, and rest at room temperature for 1 hour.

2. Preheat the oven to moderate (180°C). Lightly grease a baking tray. Roll the dough out on a lightly floured surface, stretching gently as you go, to a thin 80cm round (don't worry if the shape isn't perfect).

3. Peel and core the apples and cut each into thin slices. Combine with the sultanas, sugar and cinnamon. Arrange in a pile onto the pastry about 40cm long. Roll up to enclose and tuck ends underneath. Brush with melted butter and sprinkle with extra sugar.

4. Place onto prepared tray, and bake for about 35 minutes, until golden brown. Dust with cinnamon sugar, and serve with custard or ice-cream.

Biscuits and cookies

There would be an awful noise in our house when my kids were small if there were no biscuits in the tin! The first thing I learned to cook when I was seven years old was Anzac biscuits and I won my first competition with them that year. My eldest son, David, still loves them and says, 'Make us a batch, Mum' − and I do! Most mothers in the country would have biscuits in the tin. We had to make our own and I loved doing it. I would bake biscuits at least once a week, because when the kids came home they often brought friends. Sometimes I'd get sneaky and make a big batch and hide some away.

Merle's honey jumbles

These are extremely addictive ... be warned!

PREP TIME: 40 MINS
COOKING TIME: 8 MINS PER BATCH
MAKES ABOUT 24

125g butter, at room temperature, chopped
¾ cup caster sugar
1 egg
1 tbsp honey
½ tsp vanilla essence
2 cups self-raising flour

FILLING
1½ cups icing sugar
20g soft butter
1 tbsp honey
1 tbsp lemon juice

1. Preheat oven to moderate (180°C). Grease two large baking trays and line with baking paper.

2. Use electric beaters to cream the butter and sugar until pale. Beat in the egg, honey and vanilla, then use a butter knife to mix in the flour.

3. Roll 2 teaspoonfuls of mixture into balls. Place onto trays, leaving room for spreading, and gently flatten to 4cm rounds (you will have to shape and cook these in batches).

4. Bake for about 8 minutes, until lightly golden. Leave on trays for 5 minutes, then transfer to a wire rack to cool.

5. To make the filling, sift the icing sugar into a bowl. Add the butter, honey and lemon juice and beat with a wooden spoon until smooth and slightly creamy. Sandwich the cold biscuits with the filling.

Anzac biscuits

PREP TIME: 20 MINS
COOKING TIME: 6 MINS PER BATCH
MAKES 45

1 cup plain flour
2 tsp ground ginger
1½ cups rolled oats
1 cup desiccated coconut
1 cup white sugar
1 tbsp golden syrup
2 tbsp boiling water
1 tsp bicarb soda
160g butter, melted

I entered these into a show when I was seven, and won 1st prize! I had the competitive spirit even then.

1 Preheat oven to moderate (170°C) and grease two large baking trays.

2 Sift the flour and ground ginger into a mixing bowl, and add the oats, coconut and sugar. Make a well in the centre.

3 Stir the golden syrup, boiling water and bicarb in a small bowl until combined. Add to the dry ingredients, along with the melted butter. Mix well.

4 Take heaped teaspoons of mixture and roll into balls. Place onto trays, and flatten gently. Bake for 6–7 minutes, until lightly golden.

5 Cool on the trays for 10 minutes, until they firm up slightly, then lift onto wire racks to cool completely.

Fruit mince cookies

PREP TIME: 15 MINS
COOKING TIME: 10–12 MINS
MAKES 35

60g butter, at room temperature, chopped
¼ cup white sugar
1 egg, lightly beaten
1¼ cups plain flour
2½ tsp baking powder
½ tsp ground cinnamon
¾ cup fruit mince

Full of minced fruit, these cookies are mainly served around Christmas.

1 Preheat the oven to moderate (180°C). Lightly grease two large baking trays.

2 Use electric beaters to cream butter and sugar until white and fluffy. Add the egg and beat until combined.

3 Sift the flour, baking powder and cinnamon. Fold half into the butter mixture, then half the fruit mince, then repeat with the rest.

4 Drop heaped teaspoonfuls onto the tray, allowing room for spreading. Bake for 10–12 minutes, until golden. Leave on trays for 5 minutes, before transferring to a wire rack to cool.

Melting moments

Like most of the biscuits and cookies in this chapter, these are a favourite with the kids — they like to lick the icing from the middle!

PREP TIME: 30 MINS
COOKING TIME: 15–20 MINS
MAKES ABOUT 20

1. Preheat oven to moderately slow (160°C). Grease two large baking trays and line with baking paper.
2. Using electric beaters, cream the butter and icing sugar until pale and fluffy.
3. Sift the flours over the butter mixture, and use a butter knife to mix until evenly combined. Gather the dough together, and roll heaped teaspoons into balls. Place onto the trays, and flatten with a lightly floured fork.
4. Cook for 15–20 minutes, until lightly golden underneath. Leave on the trays for 5 minutes, then transfer to a wire rack to cool.
5. For the filling, use electric beaters to cream the butter, icing sugar and vanilla until pale and fluffy. Spread or pipe the filling onto half the biscuits and sandwich with the other half.

180g butter, at room temperature, chopped
⅔ cup icing sugar
1¼ cups plain flour
⅓ cup cornflour

FILLING
100g butter, at room temperature, chopped
¾ cup icing sugar
1 tsp vanilla essence

Coconut biscuits

PREP TIME: 20 MINS
COOKING TIME: 10–12 MINS
MAKES ABOUT 55

I went to make the original recipe for these one day but forgot to put in all the ingredients and they came out crunchy. That's how this recipe was born!

150g butter, at room temperature, chopped
1⅓ cups white sugar
1 tsp vanilla essence
1 egg
2 cups desiccated coconut
2½ cups self-raising flour
pinch of salt

1. Preheat the oven to moderate (180°C) and line two baking trays with baking paper.
2. Use electric beaters to cream the butter, sugar and vanilla until white and fluffy. Beat in the egg.
3. Use a wooden spoon to mix in the coconut, then the flour and salt. Shape heaped teaspoons of mixture into balls, and place onto the trays and flatten slightly.
4. Bake for 10–12 minutes, until lightly golden. Leave on the trays for 5 minutes to firm up, before transferring to a wire rack to cool.

NOTE: Always add the coconut before the flour, or the biscuits won't be crunchy.

Ginger nuts

PREP TIME: 20 MINS
COOKING TIME: 10–12 MINS PER BATCH
MAKES 35

40g butter, at room temperature
1 cup caster sugar
pinch of salt
1 egg
1 tbsp milk
1 tbsp golden syrup
1 tbsp treacle
2 tsp lemon juice
2 cups plain flour
½ tsp bicarb soda
1 tsp cream of tartar
1 tsp ground ginger

These are beaut to dip in your cup of tea!

1. Preheat oven to moderate (180°C). Line two baking trays with baking paper.

2. Using electric beaters, cream the butter, sugar, salt, egg and milk. Beat in the golden syrup, treacle and lemon juice.

3. Use a wooden spoon to mix in the flour sifted with the bicarb, cream of tartar and ginger. Take heaped teaspoons of the mixture and, with lightly floured hands, roll into balls.

4. Place onto trays, and flatten to 3–4cm rounds. Bake for 10–12 minutes, until golden.

5. Leave on the trays for 5 minutes to firm up, before transferring to a wire rack to cool.

Plain biscuits

PREP TIME: 20 MINS
COOKING TIME: 12–15 MINS PER BATCH
MAKES ABOUT 60

250g butter, at room temperature, chopped
1 cup white sugar
1 tsp vanilla essence
pinch of salt
1 egg
2½ cups plain flour
¼ cup cornflour
2 tbsp milk

For someone who can't eat a lot of sugar or cream-filled biscuits, these are a great standby.

1 Preheat the oven to moderately slow (160°C) and line two large baking trays with baking paper.

2 Use electric beaters to cream the butter, sugar and vanilla until white and fluffy. Beat in the salt and egg.

3 Sift the flours over the butter mixture, and add the milk. Use a butter knife to mix until evenly combined. Gather the dough together, and roll heaped teaspoons into balls. Place onto the trays, and flatten with a lightly floured fork. (You will need to cook these in batches.)

4 Cook for 12–15 minutes, until lightly golden. Transfer to a wire rack to cool.

Shortbread

I mostly make this around Christmas time and give it away as gifts. It's delicious, and you can make it into any shape you like.

PREP TIME: 20 MINS
COOKING TIME: 30–35 MINS
MAKES 8

180g butter, at room temperature, chopped
½ cup icing sugar
1⅔ cups plain flour

1. Preheat oven to slow (145°C), and lightly grease a baking tray.
2. Use electric beaters to cream the butter and icing sugar until pale and fluffy.
3. Use a butter knife to mix in the flour, then gather the dough together and press or roll out to an 18cm round. Place onto a tray and use a small teaspoon or your fingertips to decorate the edge of the dough. Score the dough into wedges and prick with a fork for decoration.
4. Bake for 30–35 minutes, until pale golden. Cool, then cut or break into wedges to serve.

NOTE: Any leftover mixture can be rolled flat and made into biscuits.

Choc-chip cookies

PREP TIME: 20 MINS
COOKING TIME: 12–15 MINS
MAKES 30

125g butter, at room temperature, chopped
1 cup white sugar
pinch of salt
1 tsp vanilla essence
1 egg
1 cup dark choc bits
2 cups self-raising flour
1 tbsp milk

1. Preheat the oven to moderately slow (160°C). Line two baking trays with baking paper.

2. Use electric beaters to cream butter and sugar until white and fluffy. Beat in the salt and vanilla, then the egg.

3. Use a butter knife then your fingers to mix in the choc bits, flour, then milk. Roll level tablespoons of the mixture into balls.

4. Place onto trays and flatten slightly. Bake for 12–15 minutes, until lightly golden. Cool on wire racks.

Oatmeal cookies

PREP TIME: 25 MINS
COOKING TIME: 10–12 MINS PER BATCH
MAKES 25

125g butter, at room temperature, chopped
1 cup brown sugar
1 egg
1½ cups plain flour
1 tsp salt
1½ tsp bicarb soda
½ tsp ground cinnamon
½ tsp ground nutmeg
¼ tsp ground cloves
⅓ cup milk
1½ cups rolled oats
¾ cup chopped walnuts
1 cup sultanas
icing sugar, to dust

1 Preheat oven to moderate (180°C). Grease two baking trays and line with baking paper.

2 Use electric beaters to cream the butter and sugar until white and fluffy. Beat in the egg.

3 Sift the flour, salt, bicarb and spices, and mix into the butter mixture with a large metal spoon. Stir in the milk and oats, then the walnuts and sultanas.

4 Drop heaped tablespoons of the mixture onto the trays and flatten slightly, leaving room for spreading. Bake for 10–12 minutes, until golden. Leave on the trays for 5 minutes, then transfer to a wire rack to cool. Dust with icing sugar.

Jam drops

PREP TIME: 30 MINS
COOKING TIME: 12–15 MINS
MAKES ABOUT 24

125g butter, at room temperature, chopped
1 cup white sugar
pinch of salt
1 tsp vanilla essence
1 egg
1¾ cups plain flour
¼ cup cornflour
1½ tsp baking powder
raspberry jam, to fill

Always popular with the kids or grandkids as they love to lick the jam from the middle before eating the biscuits.

1 Preheat the oven to moderately slow (160°C). Line two baking trays with baking paper.

2 Use electric beaters to cream butter and sugar until white and fluffy. Beat in the salt and vanilla, then the egg.

3 Use a butter knife to mix in the flour sifted with the cornflour and baking powder. Gather the dough together, and roll walnut-sized pieces into balls.

4 Place onto trays, using your finger to press an indentation into the middle of each. Fill with jam. Bake for 12–15 minutes, until very lightly golden. Cool on wire racks.

Butterscotch biscuits

1. Preheat the oven to moderate (170°C). Line two baking trays with baking paper.

2. Melt the butter in a saucepan over low heat. Stir in the brown sugar and cool slightly. Stir in the egg and vanilla.

3. Sift the dry ingredients onto the butter mixture. Mix with a butter knife until combined.

4. Place the mixture into a large piping bag fitted with a flat-sided star nozzle. Pipe the mixture into 6cm lengths onto the trays, leaving room for spreading. Bake for 10 minutes, until pale golden.

5. Leave on trays for 5 minutes, then transfer to a wire rack to cool.

PREP TIME: 20 MINS
COOKING TIME: 10 MINS
MAKES ABOUT 45

125g butter, chopped
1 cup brown sugar
1 egg, lightly beaten
½ tsp vanilla essence
1¾ cups plain flour
½ tsp bicarb soda
1 tsp cream of tartar
½ tsp salt

NOTE: If you don't want to pipe the mixture, you could roll it into balls, or use a biscuit press to shape them.

Rock cakes

PREP TIME: 20 MINS
COOKING TIME: 12–15 MINS PER BATCH
MAKES 24

125g butter, at room temperature, chopped
¾ cup white sugar
1 egg
1 tsp vanilla essence
1¼ cups self-raising flour
pinch of salt
¼ cup milk
1 cup dried mixed fruit
cornflakes, optional

My daughter Marianne's husband loves my rock cakes. Whenever I'm going to stay with them he tells me he has all the ingredients ready and waiting for me to bake a big batch.

1 Preheat the oven to moderately hot (200°C). Grease two baking trays.

2 Using electric beaters, cream the butter and sugar until white and fluffy. Beat in the egg and vanilla.

3 Mix in the sifted flour and salt with the milk and dried fruit. Drop heaped tablespoons of mixture onto the trays, or roll in cornflakes first if you like. Allow room on the trays for spreading. Bake for 12–15 minutes, until golden.

4 Transfer to a wire rack to cool.

Peanut biscuits

PREP TIME: 20 MINS
COOKING TIME: 10–12 MINS PER BATCH
MAKES 50

125g butter
½ cup white sugar
1 tsp vanilla essence
1 egg
1¼ cup self-raising flour
¾ cup chopped unsalted roasted peanuts

1. Preheat the oven to moderately slow (160°C). Line two baking trays with baking paper.

2. Use electric beaters to cream the butter, sugar and vanilla until white and fluffy. Beat in the egg.

3. Use a butter knife to mix in the flour and peanuts. Place heaped teaspoons onto the trays, leaving room for spreading. Bake for 10–12 minutes, until golden.

4. Leave on trays for 5 minutes, then transfer to a wire rack to cool.

NOTE: If you like, make these chocolate flavoured by adding 2 tbsp cocoa powder with the flour.

Slices

I didn't start making slices until I had been baking for more than ten years. They are popular now but they haven't always been the in thing. They are made from your basic four ounces of butter and sugar like a cake, but at the end they cut more than a cake, so you get more out of them. ❀ They can be a real showpiece for competitions, but I won't do them for the Royal Easter Show because you have to do three different types!

Passionfruit slice

PREP TIME: 20 MINS
COOKING TIME: 30 MINS
MAKES 20

BASE
1 cup self-raising flour
1 cup desiccated coconut
½ cup white sugar
125g butter, melted

TOPPING
395g can condensed milk
½ cup strained fresh lemon juice
⅓ cup passionfruit pulp

1. Preheat the oven to moderate (180°C). Grease a 28cm x 18cm (base measurement) slice tin and line with baking paper, hanging over the two long sides.

2. Combine the flour, coconut and sugar in a bowl. Stir in the butter and mix well. Spread into the tin; press and smooth with the back of a spoon. Bake for 15 minutes until lightly browned.

3. For the topping, combine the condensed milk, lemon juice and passionfruit pulp in a bowl and beat with a wooden spoon until smooth. Pour over the base and bake for 15 mins or until just set. Cool in the tin then lift out the slice and cut into squares to serve.

Opera House slice

PREP TIME: 25 MINS
COOKING TIME: 25 MINS
MAKES 20

BASE
¾ cup plain flour
¾ cup self-raising flour
½ cup icing sugar
125g butter, chopped

TOPPING
60g butter
½ cup white sugar
2 tsp vanilla essence
1½ tbsp milk
1¾ cups mixed dried fruit
¾ cup slivered almonds

This recipe is special to me as it is my sister-in-law Nola's. To be honest, I'm not sure where the name of the recipe comes from, but perhaps it's because of the different layers.

1. Preheat the oven to moderate (180°C). Grease a 30cm x 20cm (base measurement) slice tin and line with baking paper, hanging over the two long sides.

2. To make the base, sift the flours and icing sugar into a mixing bowl. Rub in the butter with your fingertips until evenly combined. Press into the tin, and bake for 15 minutes.

3. For the topping, melt the butter in a saucepan, and add the sugar, vanilla, milk and fruit. Stir over low heat until the sugar has dissolved. Remove from heat and stir in the almonds.

4. Spread over the base, and cook for 10 minutes until the almonds are lightly golden. Cool in the tin, then lift out and cut into squares to serve.

Rice Bubble slice

PREP TIME: 15 MINS
COOKING TIME: 5 MINS + 30 MINS SETTING
MAKES 25

125g butter
1 cup brown sugar
1⅔ cups chopped dates
3 cups Rice Bubbles

Needless to say, this is a very popular one with the kids!

1. Grease a 26cm x 16cm (base measurement) slice tin and line the base with baking paper, hanging over the two long sides.

2. Melt the butter in a saucepan. Add the sugar and dates and stir well. Bring to the boil, reduce the heat slightly and simmer for 5 minutes.

3. Add the Rice Bubbles and stir to combine. Spread into the tin; press and smooth with the back of a spoon. Refrigerate for 30 minutes or until set.

4. Lift out of the tin, and cut into squares to serve.

Chocolate almond slice

1. Lay a sheet of greaseproof paper (or baking paper) on a tray. Arrange 12 biscuits in three rows of four, close together. Combine the milk and almond essence, and brush some of it onto the biscuits.

2. Place the cream, rum and all but about 1½ tbsp of the milk mixture into a bowl. Sprinkle the pudding mix on top, and use electric beaters to beat for 1 minute. Spread evenly onto the biscuits, taking care not to move them. Place the remaining biscuits on top, arranged in the same way as the bottom layer. Brush with the reserved milk mixture.

3. For the topping, combine the chocolate, butter, milk and sifted cocoa in a saucepan, and stir over medium heat until melted and smooth. Transfer to a bowl and stand for about 30 minutes, until cooled and thickened slightly, then spread over the slice. Leave until set, then cover and refrigerate overnight so the biscuits soften slightly.

4. Cut into portions, using a large, sharp knife.

PREP TIME: 20 MINS
COOKING TIME: 2 MINS
+ OVERNIGHT SETTING
MAKES 12

24 Milk Coffee biscuits
½ cup milk
1 tsp almond essence
300ml cream
1 tbsp rum
100g pkt vanilla instant pudding mix

TOPPING
125g dark chocolate, chopped
90g butter
2 tbsp milk
¼ cup cocoa powder

Quick slice

PREP TIME: 10 MINS
COOKING TIME: 15–20 MINS
MAKES 18

175g butter, melted
250g plain sweet biscuits, roughly crushed
1 cup roughly chopped walnuts
½ cup chopped glacé ginger
½ cup chopped glacé cherries
½ cup desiccated coconut
½ cup choc bits
395g can condensed milk

If you're in a hurry this is the perfect slice to make. Hence its name!

1. Preheat oven to moderate (170°C). Grease a 28cm x 18cm (base measurement) slice tin and line with baking paper, hanging over the two long sides.

2. Mix the butter and biscuits together and press into the tin. Sprinkle with the walnuts, ginger, cherries, coconut and choc bits.

3. Drizzle the condensed milk over, and bake for 15–20 minutes, until browned. Leave for about 1 hour to cool. Cut into squares to serve.

Date slice

PREP TIME: 20 MINS
COOKING TIME: 20–25 MINS
MAKES 25

125g butter, chopped
1 cup brown sugar
1 cup chopped dates
1 egg, lightly beaten
1 cup walnuts
1 cup self-raising flour
pinch of salt
icing sugar to dust

1. Preheat the oven to moderately hot (190°C). Grease a 30cm x 20cm (base measurement) slice tin and line with baking paper, hanging over the two long sides.

2. Melt the butter in a large saucepan, and remove from the heat. Stir in the sugar and dates, then the egg. Mix in the walnuts, then fold in the sifted flour and salt.

3. Spread into the tin, and smooth the surface. Bake for 20–25 minutes, until golden brown. Cool in the tin, dust lightly with icing sugar, then cut into squares to serve.

Date and ginger slice

PREP TIME: 15 MINS
+ 30 MINS CHILLING
COOKING TIME: 5 MINS
MAKES 16

BASE

125g butter, chopped
⅓ cup white sugar
1 cup chopped dates
¼ cup chopped glacé ginger
3 cups Special K

TOPPING

250g dark chocolate, chopped

1. Grease a 26cm x 16cm (base measurement) slice tin and line with baking paper, hanging over the two long sides.

2. Melt the butter and sugar together in a large saucepan. Stir in the dates and ginger, to soften slightly.

3. Remove from the heat and stir in the Special K. Spread into the tin; press and smooth with the back of a spoon. Refrigerate for 30 minutes, until firm.

4. Place the chocolate into a heatproof bowl and stand over a saucepan of just simmering water (make sure the bottom of the bowl doesn't touch the water). Leave until the chocolate is starting to melt, then stir until smooth.

5. Spread the chocolate over the slice, and leave to set. Lift out of the tin, and cut into squares to serve.

Banana slice

1. Preheat oven to moderate (180°C). Grease a 30cm x 20cm (base measurement) slice tin and line with baking paper, hanging over the two long sides.

2. Using a wooden spoon, mix together the cake mix, butter and egg. Spread into the tin and smooth the surface with the back of a spoon. Bake for 15 minutes, until springy to a gentle touch. Set aside to cool.

3. Combine the chilled condensed milk and the lemon juice. Whip the cream and fold into the condensed milk mixture. Quickly spread over the base, and refrigerate overnight. Cut into squares to serve.

PREP TIME: 15 MINS
+ OVERNIGHT CHILLING
COOKING TIME: 15 MINS
MAKES 20

BASE
430g pkt banana cake mix
40g butter, at room temperature
1 egg

TOPPING
395g can condensed milk, chilled
⅓ cup lemon juice
300ml thickened cream

NOTE: Use a cake mix close to the size given if you can't find that exact one.

Coffee walnut slice

PREP TIME: 20 MINS
 + OVERNIGHT CHILLING
COOKING TIME: 5 MINS
MAKES 15

250g Milk Coffee biscuits
125g Copha, chopped
2 cups desiccated coconut
½ cup chopped walnuts
2 tbsp cocoa powder
200ml condensed milk
2 tsp vanilla essence
⅔ cup walnut pieces, to decorate

COFFEE ICING
2 cups icing sugar mixture
2 tsp instant coffee powder
2 tbsp boiling water

1. Grease a 28cm x 18cm (base measurement) slice tin and line with baking paper, hanging over the two long sides. Line the base of the tin with a single layer of biscuits, trimming to fit as necessary.

2. Melt the Copha in a large saucepan over low heat, then set aside to cool. Add the coconut, walnuts, cocoa powder, condensed milk and vanilla. Mix well.

3. Press the mixture over the biscuit base, then top with another layer of biscuits, pressing down firmly. Refrigerate overnight.

4. To make the coffee icing, sift the icing sugar into a bowl. Dissolve the coffee powder in the water. Add to the icing sugar, and stir until smooth. Spread onto the slice, decorate with walnut pieces, and leave to set.

Caramel slice

PREP TIME: 30 MINS
COOKING TIME: 35 MINS
MAKES 20

BASE

½ cup brown sugar
1 cup self-raising flour
1 cup desiccated coconut
125g butter, melted and cooled
1 egg, lightly beaten
1 tsp vanilla essence
pinch of salt

FILLING

395g can condensed milk
2 tbsp golden syrup
1 tbsp butter

TOPPING

200g dark chocolate, melted

This is my favourite slice. It's my mum's recipe and works every time.

1 Preheat the oven to moderate (180°C). Grease a 28cm x 18cm (base measurement) slice tin and line with baking paper, hanging over the two long sides.

2 Combine the dry ingredients in a large mixing bowl and make a well in the centre. Add the butter, egg, vanilla and salt. Mix with a wooden spoon until combined. Press evenly into the tin, using the back of a spoon to smooth the surface. Bake for 15 minutes.

3 Reduce oven to slow (150C). Combine the filling ingredients in a small saucepan, and stir until melted and smooth. Pour over the base and bake for 20 minutes. Cool.

4 Place the chocolate in a heatproof bowl and stand over a saucepan of just simmering water (make sure the bottom of the bowl doesn't touch the water). Leave until the chocolate is starting to melt, then stir until smooth.

5 Spread the melted chocolate over the slice, and refrigerate for 20 minutes, to set. Cut into squares to serve.

Coconut slice

PREP TIME: 15 MINS
COOKING TIME: 10–15 MINS
MAKES 15

BASE

1½ cups self-raising flour
1 cup desiccated coconut
½ cup brown sugar
150g butter, melted
1 tsp vanilla essence
lemon zest, to decorate, optional

LEMON ICING

2 cups icing sugar mixture
¼ cup strained lemon juice

This is one of my daughter Marianne's favourites.

1 Preheat the oven to moderate (180°C). Grease a 30cm x 20cm (base measurement) slice tin and line with baking paper, hanging over the two long sides.

2 Combine the flour, coconut and sugar in a mixing bowl, and make a well in the centre. Add the melted butter and vanilla and mix until evenly combined.

3 Spread into the tin; press and smooth with the back of a spoon. Bake for 10–15 minutes, until golden. Set aside to cool.

4 For the lemon icing, sift the icing sugar into a bowl and mix in the lemon juice until smooth. Spread over the slice, and leave to set. Cut into squares. Decorate with lemon zest if you like.

Vanilla slice

1. Preheat the oven to moderately hot (200°C), and lightly grease two large baking trays. Place a sheet of pastry onto each tray, and use a fork to prick all over. Bake for 10 minutes, until golden brown. Leave to cool.

2. Heat the milk in a saucepan until it is just about to boil. Whisk the egg, sugar and cornflour in a bowl until pale, then slowly pour the hot milk in, still whisking. Pour back into the saucepan. Stir over medium heat for about 5 minutes, until the mixture thickens. Take it off the heat and stir in the butter. Let the custard cool until just warm, then stir in the vanilla.

3. Grease a 20cm square (base measurement) cake tin and line with baking paper, hanging over two of the sides. Trim the cooked pastry sheets so they will fit snugly, and place one piece into the tin. Spread the custard over. Place the remaining pastry sheet on top, flat side up. Refrigerate overnight.

4. To make the icing, sift the icing sugar into a bowl. Add the passionfruit pulp, and stir until smooth. Spread over the pastry, and leave for 15 minutes to set. Lift out of the tin, and cut into squares.

**PREP TIME: 30 MINS
+ OVERNIGHT CHILLING
COOKING TIME: 15 MINS
MAKES 16**

2 sheets frozen butter puff pastry, thawed
1½ cups milk
1 egg, lightly beaten
1 heaped tbsp white sugar
1 heaped tbsp cornflour
1 tbsp butter
1 tsp vanilla essence

ICING
1½ cups icing sugar mixture
¼ cup passionfruit pulp

Peanut slice

PREP TIME: 15 MINS
COOKING TIME: 20 MINS
MAKES 24

1 cup self-raising flour
1 cup brown sugar
1 cup desiccated coconut
1 cup cornflakes
150g butter, melted
1 tsp vanilla essence
2 tbsp milk
½ cup chopped unsalted roasted peanuts

1 Preheat the oven to moderate (180°C). Grease a 30cm x 20cm (base measurement) slice tin and line with baking paper, hanging over the two long sides.

2 Combine the flour, sugar, coconut and cornflakes in a mixing bowl and make a well in the centre.

3 Pour in the butter, vanilla and milk. Mix together – if it looks a little bit dry add a little extra milk. Spread into the tin; press the peanuts on top. Bake for 20 minutes, until golden. Cool in the tin for 30 minutes, then lift out to cool completely. Cut into squares to serve.

Rolled oat slice

PREP TIME: 20 MINS
COOKING TIME: 20 MINS
MAKES 20

2 cups rolled oats
½ cup brown sugar
½ cup desiccated coconut
1 cup plain flour
1 tsp baking powder
150g butter, melted
2 tbsp honey

1. Preheat the oven to moderate (180°C). Grease a 28cm x 18cm (base measurement) slice tin and line with baking paper, hanging over the two long sides.

2. Combine the oats, sugar and coconut in a mixing bowl. Sift the flour and baking powder over, and make a well in the centre.

3. Pour the butter and honey over and stir to evenly combine. Press into the tin, and bake for 20 minutes, until lightly golden. Cool in the tin, then cut into squares to serve.

Marshmallow slice

PREP TIME: 30 MINS
COOKING TIME: 20 MINS
MAKES 16

'Yum' is all my friends say whenever this is mentioned. The grandkids always like to help with this and then I have to clean up after them!

BASE

3 Weetbix, crushed (or 2 cups Rice Bubbles)
½ cup brown sugar
pinch of salt
1 cup desiccated coconut
1 cup self-raising flour
250g Copha, melted

MARSHMALLOW TOPPING

1 cup white sugar
1 tbsp gelatine powder
1 cup water

NOTE: Use a hot knife to cut the slice. Dip into hot water and dry before each cut.

1. Preheat the oven to moderate (170°C). Grease a 28cm x 18cm (base measurement) slice tin and line with baking paper, hanging over the two long sides.

2. For the base, combine the dry ingredients in a mixing bowl and make a well in the centre. Pour in the Copha, and stir until evenly combined. Spread into the tin; press and smooth with the back of a spoon. Bake for 20 minutes. Set aside to cool.

3. To make the marshmallow topping, combine the sugar, gelatine and water in a saucepan. Stir over low heat without boiling until the sugar dissolves, then increase the heat to medium and bring to the boil. Cook for 5 minutes, then transfer to a bowl to cool.

4. Use electric beaters to beat the mixture until it is thick and makes stiff peaks. Spread over the base, and leave for 30 minutes to set. Lift out of the tin and cut into bars to serve.

Chocolate fudge slice

1. Grease a 20cm square (base measurement) cake tin and line with baking paper, hanging over two sides.

2. Combine the butter, sugar, milk, vanilla, cocoa powder and walnuts in a saucepan and bring to the boil.

3. Cool, then stir in the Milk Arrowroot biscuits. Spoon into the tin; press and smooth with the back of a spoon. Refrigerate for 1 hour, until set.

4. For the topping, melt the chocolate and butter together in a saucepan over low heat. Cool for 15 minutes, until thickened slightly.

5. Lift the slice out of the tin, and spread with topping. Leave to set, then cut into diamonds.

PREP TIME: 20 MINS
+ 1 HOUR CHILLING
COOKING TIME: 5 MINS
MAKES ABOUT 24

90g butter
½ cup white sugar
3½ tbs milk
1 tsp vanilla essence
1 tbsp cocoa powder
½ cup chopped walnuts
250g Milk Arrowroot biscuits, crushed

TOPPING
200g dark chocolate
60g butter

VARIATION: Use sultanas instead of walnuts if you like.

Arrowroot biscuit slice

PREP TIME: 15 MINS
COOKING TIME: 2 MINS
MAKES 20

250g Milk Arrowroot biscuits
1 cup mixed dried fruit
125g butter, chopped
½ cup brown sugar
2 tbsp honey

ICING
1½ cups icing sugar
1 tsp vanilla essence
2 tsp coffee powder
3 tsp boiling water

1 Grease a 26cm x 16cm (base measurement) slice tin and line the base with baking paper, hanging over the two long sides.

2 Finely crush the biscuits and place into a large bowl with the dried fruit. Make a well in the centre.

3 Place the butter, sugar and honey in a small saucepan and cook over low heat until melted and smooth. Pour into the dry ingredients, and mix until evenly combined.

4 Spread into the tin; press and smooth with the back of a spoon. Refrigerate for 2 hours, until set.

5 To make the icing, combine icing sugar, vanilla essence, coffee powder and boiling water until smooth. Spread over the slice and leave to set. Lift out and cut into squares to serve.

Chocolate fruit slice

PREP TIME: 20 MINS
COOKING TIME: 20 MINS
MAKES 16

125g butter, at room temperature, chopped
½ cup white sugar
½ tsp vanilla essence
1 egg
½ cup self-raising flour
½ cup plain flour
1 tbsp cocoa powder
1 cup mixed dried fruit
¼ cup milk

1 Preheat the oven to moderate (180°C). Grease a 28cm x 18cm (base measurement) slice tin and line with baking paper, hanging over the two long sides.

2 Use electric beaters to cream the butter, sugar and vanilla until white and fluffy. Add the egg and beat well.

3 Stir in the sifted flours and cocoa powder, fruit and milk. Spread into the tin and bake for 20 minutes until springy to a gentle touch in the middle. Cool in the tin, then lift out and cut into fingers to serve.

Caramel fingers

PREP TIME: 20 MINS
COOKING TIME: 25 MINS
MAKES 15

150g butter
½ cup brown sugar
1 tsp vanilla essence
1 egg
¾ cup chopped dates
½ cup chopped walnuts
1 cup self-raising flour

CARAMEL ICING
¼ cup brown sugar
¼ cup icing sugar, sifted
30g softened butter
1 tbsp boiling water

1. Preheat the oven to moderate (180°C). Grease a 30cm x 20cm (base measurement) slice tin and line with baking paper, hanging over the two long sides.

2. Using electric beaters, cream the butter, sugar and vanilla until pale. Add the egg and beat until combined.

3. Fold in the dates and walnuts, then the flour. Spread into the tin and smooth the surface with the back of a spoon.

4. Bake for 20–25 minutes, until golden. Leave in the tin to cool completely.

5. To make the icing, combine the sugars in a bowl. Add the butter and water and stir until smooth. Drizzle over the slice, leave to set, then lift out of the tin and cut into fingers to serve.

Macadamia fudge fingers

1. Grease a 28cm x 18cm (base measurement) slice tin and line with baking paper, hanging over the two long sides.

2. Combine the biscuits, coconut, cocoa and macadamias in a large mixing bowl and make a well in the centre.

3. Pour in the condensed milk and melted butter, and stir until combined. Press into the tin and smooth with the back of a spoon. Refrigerate for 2 hours.

4. Melt the dark and white choc melts separately, and put into two small piping bags with a small hole snipped across the corner, or fitted with a narrow nozzle. Lift slice out of the tin and cut into fingers. Pipe dark chocolate across the slice one way, then white chocolate the other. Leave for 5–10 minutes to set.

**PREP TIME: 20 MINS
 + 2 HOURS CHILLING
MAKES 15**

250g plain sweet biscuits, crushed
1 cup desiccated coconut
½ cup cocoa powder
1¼ cups chopped macadamias
395g can condensed milk
60g butter, melted
½ cup dark choc melts
½ cup white choc melts

Raspberry slice

PREP TIME: 30 MINS
COOKING TIME: 35 MINS
MAKES 12

BASE

90g butter, at room temperature
½ cup white sugar
pinch of salt
1 tsp vanilla essence
1 egg
⅔ cup plain flour
⅓ cup self-raising flour
½ cup raspberry jam

TOPPING

2 eggs, lightly beaten
⅓ cup white sugar
2 cups desiccated coconut

1. Preheat oven to moderately slow (160°C). Grease a 28cm x 18cm (base measurement) slice tin and line with baking paper, hanging over the two long sides.

2. Use electric beaters to cream the butter, sugar, salt and vanilla together until white and fluffy, then beat in the egg. Mix in the sifted flours, and press evenly into the tin, using the back of a spoon to smooth the surface. Bake for 15 minutes.

3. Spread jam over the base. Combine the topping ingredients and spread over the jam. Bake for a further 20 minutes, until golden. Cool, then cut into squares to serve.

Morning and afternoon tea

Morning and afternoon tea are not competition categories, but at the CWA we have them as get-togethers. The host might supply all the food, or the members might bring along a contribution, depending on the event. Each year the members of the CWA study a different country, then we have an International Day at the end with a big morning tea. School children get involved as well and make posters to decorate the room. We try to include a dish from the country we have just studied, but recently the country was Iceland. Which proved a little difficult!

Spiced fruit loaf

PREP TIME: 20 MINS + COOLING + OVERNIGHT SOAKING
COOKING TIME: 1 HOUR 10 MINS
SERVES 12

¾ cup chopped dates
⅔ cup chopped dried apricots
2 tbsp brandy (or other spirit)
⅔ cup raw sugar (or white sugar)
125g butter, at room temperature, chopped
½ tsp bicarb soda
¾ cup boiling water
2 eggs, lightly beaten
¾ cup wholemeal self-raising flour
¾ cup wholemeal plain flour
1 tsp mixed spice
⅔ cup chopped salted cashews (optional)
¼ cup desiccated coconut

1 Combine the fruit and brandy in a large mixing bowl, cover and stand overnight.

2 Preheat the oven to moderately slow (160°C). Grease a 23cm x 12cm (base measurement) loaf tin and line with baking paper, hanging over the two long sides of the tin.

3 Add the sugar, butter and bicarb to the fruit, then pour over the boiling water. Mix together then leave to cool, stirring occasionally to release the heat. Stir in the eggs.

4 Sift the dry ingredients over the mixture, and return the husks. Fold together until just combined, along with the cashews and coconut. Bake for 1 hour 10 minutes, until firm to a gentle touch in the centre. Cool in the tin for 10 minutes, then lift out, remove paper and cool on a wire rack.

NOTE: To cut the fruit, use lightly oiled scissors, and try to make sure the pieces are the same size – quite small.

Delicious pikelets

PREP TIME: 15 MINS
COOKING TIME: 3 MINS PER BATCH
MAKES ABOUT 20

1 cup self-raising flour
½ tsp salt
2 tbsp white sugar
1 egg
150ml milk
butter, to grease
jam and butter or cream

NOTE: Serve warm or at room temperature with jam and butter, or cream if you prefer.

1. Sift the flour and salt together into a mixing bowl, then add the sugar. Make a well in the centre. Whisk the egg and milk until combined, then pour gradually onto the dry ingredients, stirring constantly to make a smooth batter.

2. Preheat a large heavy-based frying pan over medium heat, and lightly grease. Use a dessert spoon to drop batter into the pan, allowing room for spreading (you'll probably cook about 6 per batch, depending on the size of your pan).

3. Cook for about 2 minutes, until browned underneath, then use a knife to turn over and cook the other side for about 1 minute. Cover a wire rack with a clean tea towel, and place the cooked pikelets onto it.

Lemon tart

PREP TIME: 20 MINS
COOKING TIME: 20 MINS
SERVES 6–8

BASE

200g plain sweet biscuits
100g butter, melted

FILLING

125g cream cheese, at room temperature, chopped
395g can condensed milk
2 egg yolks
½ cup lemon juice
1 tbsp finely grated lemon rind

1. Preheat oven to moderately slow (160°C). Crush the biscuits finely. Add the melted butter and mix well. Press into the base and sides of a 20cm (base measurement) pie dish. Chill while you make the filling.

2. For the filling, use electric beaters to beat the cream cheese until creamy. Beat in the condensed milk, then the egg yolks, lemon juice and rind. Pour into the base.

3. Bake for 20 minutes, until set. Cool before serving.

Lamingtons

These seem to be the most popular of all the small cakes. I've certainly made a few of these in my time!

PREP TIME: 40 MINS
COOKING TIME: 40 MINS
 + OVERNIGHT FREEZING
MAKES 24

250g butter, at room temperature, chopped
1½ cups caster sugar
4 eggs
1 tsp vanilla essence
2½ cups self-raising flour
2 tbsp cornflour
1 tsp baking powder
pinch of salt
½ cup milk, approximately

ICING

2 cups icing sugar
2 tbsp cocoa powder
90g soft butter
1 tsp vanilla essence
5 tbsp hot water
3 cups desiccated coconut, approximately

1. Preheat the oven to moderately slow (160°C). Grease a large rectangular tin (31cm x 21cm x 4.5cm deep, base measurement) and line the base with baking paper, hanging over the two long sides.

2. Using electric beaters, cream the butter and sugar until pale. Add the eggs one at a time, beating well after each addition. Beat in the vanilla.

3. Sift the flour, cornflour, baking powder and salt onto the butter mixture, and add the milk. Fold together until evenly combined. If it seems too thick, add a little bit more milk. Spread into the tin and smooth the surface. Bake for 40 minutes, until it springs back to a gentle touch in the centre.

4. Turn out onto a wire rack to cool completely. Wrap tightly in plastic wrap, and freeze for 24 hours.

5. For the icing, sift the icing sugar and cocoa powder into a large bowl. Add the butter and vanilla, then pour hot water, a little at a time, onto the butter to melt it. Stir until smooth and runny.

6. Remove the cake from the freezer and unwrap. Lay on a sheet of baking paper, and cover the top with icing. Sprinkle with coconut. Lay a sheet of baking paper over the iced surface and quickly turn the cake over. Ice and sprinkle coconut on the other side.

7. Cut into lengths about 5cm wide. Ice the cut sides and sprinkle with coconut. Cut each length into cubes. Ice the cut sides and sprinkle with coconut. Leave to set.

Raspberry coconut tarts

PREP TIME: 30 MINS
COOKING TIME: 15 MINS
MAKES 12

125g butter, at room temperature
2 tbsp white sugar
1 egg yolk
1¼ cups plain flour
1 tsp baking powder
pinch of salt

FILLING
1 egg
½ cup white sugar
¼ cup milk
1 cup desiccated coconut
raspberry jam

1 Preheat the oven to moderate (180°C). Grease a 12-hole medium muffin tin.

2 Use electric beaters to cream the butter and sugar until white and fluffy. Add the egg yolk and beat well.

3 Use a butter knife to mix in the sifted flour, baking powder and salt.

4 Gather the dough together and roll out on a lightly floured surface. Use an 8cm cutter to cut out 12 rounds of pastry, and ease into the tins.

5 For the filling, whisk the egg, sugar and milk together, then stir in the coconut. Spoon into the pastry cases, and press a little jam on top.

6 Bake for 15 minutes, until lightly golden. Cool to room temperature before serving.

Gingerbread

PREP TIME: 25 MINS
COOKING TIME: 1 HOUR
MAKES 24

125g butter, chopped
½ cup treacle
¼ cup golden syrup
½ cup milk
2 cups plain flour
1 tbsp ground ginger
1 tsp mixed spice
1 tsp bicarb soda
¼ tsp salt
2 eggs, lightly beaten

LEMON ICING
1¼ cups icing sugar mixture
2 tbsp strained lemon juice

1 Preheat the oven to slow (150°C). Grease a 20cm square cake tin, and line the base with baking paper, hanging over two sides.

2 Combine the butter, treacle, golden syrup and milk in a saucepan and heat, stirring occasionally, until the butter has melted and the mixture is smooth.

3 Sift the dry ingredients into a large bowl, and make a well in the centre. Pour in the butter mixture and the eggs, and gently stir to combine. Pour into the tin, and bake for 1 hour, until a skewer inserted into the centre comes out clean. Leave in tin to cool completely. Once cool lift out of tin.

4 Combine the icing ingredients and stir until smooth, then spread over the top. Leave to set, then cut into slices to serve.

Mum's brownie

PREP TIME: 20 MINS
COOKING TIME: 35–40 MINS
MAKES 20

1 cup white sugar
125g butter, chopped
1 cup water
1 tsp bicarb soda
1 heaped cup mixed dried fruit
½ cup chopped dates
½ cup chopped nuts (see note)
2 eggs, lightly beaten
2 cups plain flour
1 tsp baking powder
melted chocolate, optional

This is quite different from the brownies we're used to these days, but it's delicious. The dates add something special to it.

1. Preheat the oven to moderate (180°C). Grease a 28cm x 18cm slice tin and line with baking paper, hanging over the two long sides.

2. Combine the sugar, butter, water, bicarb and mixed dried fruit in a saucepan, and bring to the boil. Cook over medium heat for 5 minutes. Set aside to cool.

3. Stir in the dates, nuts, eggs, sifted flour and baking powder. Pour into the tin, and bake for 35–40 minutes, until firm to a gentle touch in the centre.

4. Cool in the tin, then cut into squares to serve. Drizzle with melted chocolate, if you like.

NOTE: Use any nuts you like, such as walnuts, pecans or almonds.

Kisses

1. Preheat oven to moderately slow (160°C). Line two baking trays with baking paper.

2. Use electric beaters to cream butter, sugar, vanilla and salt until white and fluffy. Add eggs one at a time, beating well after adding.

3. Use a butter knife to mix in the sifted flour and cornflour. Transfer mixture to a piping bag fitted with a star nozzle, or use a biscuit press. Pipe shapes onto the trays, leaving room for spreading (you will need to cook these in batches). Refrigerate for 15 minutes.

4. Add a cherry quarter on top of each, and bake for 10 minutes or until pale golden. Leave on the trays for 10 minutes, then transfer to a wire rack to cool.

PREP TIME: 30 MINS
COOKING TIME: 10 MINS PER BATCH
MAKES ABOUT 60

250g butter, at room temperature, chopped
¾ cup white sugar
1 tsp vanilla essence
pinch of salt
2 eggs
2 cups self-raising flour
½ cup cornflour
¼ cup glacé cherries, quartered

Date and walnut loaf

PREP TIME: 20 MINS
COOKING TIME: 45–60 MINS
SERVES 6

1 cup chopped dates
¾ cup warm water
125g butter, at room temperature
125g white sugar
1 egg
1 tsp vanilla essence
90g chopped walnuts
1½ cups plain flour
1¼ tsp baking powder
pinch of salt

1. Preheat the oven to moderately slow (160°C). Grease a 19cm x 9cm (base measurement) loaf tin and line with baking paper, hanging over the two long sides. Soak the dates in the warm water while you prepare the other ingredients.

2. Use electric beaters to cream the butter and sugar until white and fluffy. Add the egg and vanilla, and beat until combined.

3. Fold in the dates (and water) and walnuts. Sift the flour, baking powder and salt over, and fold in until combined. Spoon into the tin, and smooth the surface. Bake for 45 minutes to 1 hour until springy to a gentle touch.

4. Stand in the tin for 5 minutes to cool slightly, then turn out onto a wire rack to cool.

Coconut ice

PREP TIME: 15 MINS
SETTING TIME: 1 HOUR
MAKES 25

3 cups icing sugar
3 cups desiccated coconut
1 tsp vanilla essence
2 egg whites, lightly beaten
125g Copha, melted and cooled slightly
pink food colouring

I make this and sell it on CWA stalls. It's a crowd-pleaser and a bestseller!

1. Grease a 20cm square cake tin, and line with baking paper, hanging over two sides.

2. Sift the icing sugar into a bowl and mix in the coconut. Make a well in the centre.

3. Add the vanilla, egg whites and Copha, and mix until evenly combined. Divide the mixture into two portions. Tint half the mixture with a few drops of pink food colouring.

4. Spread the white mixture into the tin and smooth the surface. Top with the pink mixture to make two layers. Refrigerate for 1 hour, or until set. Cut into small squares to serve.

Honey bubbles

PREP TIME: 15 MINS
+ 15 MINS CHILLING
COOKING TIME: 5 MINS
MAKES 36

4 cups Rice Bubbles
1 cup desiccated coconut
125g butter
½ cup caster sugar
2 tbsp honey

VARIATION: Drizzle with melted chocolate.

This is my sister-in-law Nola's great recipe.

1. Combine the Rice Bubbles and coconut in a large mixing bowl and make a well in the centre.

2. Melt the butter, sugar and honey in a saucepan until evenly combined and bubbling. Pour into the mixture, and mix well. Spoon into patty cases and refrigerate for 15 minutes, to set.

Honey toffee

1. Put 12 paper patty cases into patty tins or medium muffin tins. Combine the ingredients (except the hundreds and thousands) in a small saucepan and stir over low heat without boiling until the sugar dissolves.

2. Increase the heat to medium and bring to the boil, then cook for about 15 minutes, until it is dark golden brown and has reached setting stage. To test if the toffee is ready, drop a tiny bit into a cup of cold water. If it sets hard almost immediately, the toffee is ready. Alternatively, use a sugar thermometer and cook until it reaches hard crack stage.

3. Remove from the heat and let most of the bubbles subside. Pour the toffee carefully into patty cases, and leave for 15 minutes, until cool and set hard. If you want to decorate with hundreds and thousands, sprinkle on before the toffee sets.

PREP TIME: 10 MINS
COOKING TIME: 15 MINS
MAKES 12

⅔ cup white sugar
40g butter
⅓ cup honey
⅓ cup white vinegar
hundreds and thousands, optional

NOTE: Be very careful making toffee, as the mixture gets extremely hot.

Cream puffs

PREP TIME: 30 MINS
COOKING TIME: 20–25 MINS
MAKES 15

1 tbsp butter
1 cup water
1 cup self-raising flour
4 eggs, lightly beaten
150ml cream
1 tbsp icing sugar, plus extra to dust

What can I say? These are fabulous with whipped cream or jelly custard. Packed with calories!

1. Preheat the oven to moderate (180°C). Line two large baking trays with non-stick baking paper.

2. Combine the butter and water in a large saucepan, and heat until the butter melts and the mixture comes to the boil. Sift the flour into the pan, and stir with a wooden spoon over the heat for about 1 minute, until the mixture comes away from the sides of the pan in a lump.

3. Transfer the mixture to a bowl and cool slightly, stirring to release the heat. Add the eggs a little bit at a time, beating well with electric beaters between each addition, until the mixture is very thick and glossy.

4. Drop tablespoons of the mixture onto the prepared trays, leaving room for spreading. Bake for 20–25 minutes, until puffed and golden brown. Transfer to a wire rack to cool.

5. Beat the cream with the icing sugar to soft peaks. Fill the puffs with the cream, and dust with extra icing sugar. Serve immediately.

Custard tarts

PREP TIME: 25 MINS
COOKING TIME: 20–25 MINS
MAKES 24

PASTRY

1¾ cups plain flour
2 tbsp self-raising flour
¼ tsp salt
½ cup white sugar
150g cold butter, chopped
1 egg, lightly beaten

FILLING

2 tbsp caster sugar
2 tsp plain flour
2 eggs
1 cup milk
1 tsp vanilla essence
nutmeg, to sprinkle

1. Preheat the oven to moderately slow (160°C). Grease three 12-hole round-bottomed patty tins.

2. Sift the flours and salt into a bowl and stir in the sugar. Use your fingertips to rub the butter in until the mixture resembles breadcrumbs. Add the egg and mix in with a butter knife until evenly combined.

3. Gather the dough together and roll out on a lightly floured surface to 3mm thick. Use a 7cm cutter to cut out rounds of pastry, and ease into the tins.

4. For the filling, whisk the sugar, flour and eggs together, then heat the milk until boiling and pour onto the mixture while whisking. Stir in the vanilla. Transfer to a jug and pour into each pastry case. Sprinkle lightly with nutmeg.

5. Bake for 20–25 minutes, until the custard is set and the pastry is lightly golden. Cool to room temperature before serving. Sprinkle with nutmeg if you like.

Meringues

PREP TIME: 30 MINS
COOKING TIME: 1½ HOURS
MAKES ABOUT 50

3 egg whites
pinch of salt
¾ cup caster sugar

1. Preheat oven to very slow (100°C). Grease two large baking trays and line with baking paper.

2. Use electric beaters to beat the egg whites with a pinch of salt until stiff peaks form. Add sugar a tablespoon at a time, beating until the sugar has dissolved between each addition.

3. Keep adding and beating until the mixture is thick, white and glossy. Transfer to a piping bag fitted with a medium-sized fluted nozzle. Pipe rosettes of meringue onto the trays.

4. Bake for 1½ hours, then turn off the oven, prop the door open slightly and leave to cool completely.

MERINGUE HINTS AND TIPS:

- For best results, use egg whites at room temperature.
- Beaters and bowls must be very clean and dry – any grease or water can prevent the egg whites from whipping up properly.
- If the sugar is added too quickly and doesn't dissolve properly, the meringues will crack and weep during cooking, which doesn't look very nice.
- Don't try to make meringues on wet or very humid days, as the sugar absorbs moisture from the air.
- If you don't want to pipe shapes, you can spoon meringue onto the trays. Use another spoon to scrape the mixture off the first spoon.
- Sandwich the meringues with melted chocolate, or with whipped cream and/or lemon curd, close to serving time.
- Tint the meringue with food colouring, if you like.
- Meringues will keep for days stored in an airtight container.

Date shortbread

Always very popular with young and old. This is another of my mum's recipes. I couldn't tell you how many times we've both made this, but I always have it as a good old standby.

PREP TIME: 20 MINS
 + 1 HOUR COOLING
COOKING TIME: 30–40 MINS
MAKES 20

125g butter, at room temperature, chopped
½ cup white sugar
1 egg
2 cups self-raising flour
2 tbsp milk
icing sugar, to dust

FILLING

500g chopped dates
125g butter, chopped
⅓ cup water

1. Preheat the oven to moderately slow (160°C). Grease a 28cm x 18cm (base measurement) slice tin and line with baking paper, hanging over the two long sides.

2. For the filling, combine the dates, butter and water in a saucepan and simmer over low heat for about 3 minutes, until thick and soft like jam. Transfer to a bowl and set aside for about 1 hour, to cool completely.

3. Use electric beaters to cream the butter and sugar until white and fluffy. Beat in the egg. Add the flour and milk and use a butter knife to mix until combined, then gather the dough together.

4. Divide the dough into two portions, and press one portion into the tin. Spread the filling over the pastry, then use a lightly floured hand to press the remaining pastry on top. Cook for 30–40 minutes, until golden. Cool, then cut into squares. Dust with icing sugar to serve.

Chocolate éclairs

PREP TIME: 30 MINS
COOKING TIME: 20–25 MINS
MAKES 12

1 tbsp butter
1 cup water
1 cup self-raising flour
4 eggs, lightly beaten
150ml cream, whipped

CHOCOLATE ICING

1½ cups icing sugar
1 tbsp cocoa powder
1 tsp melted butter
½ tsp vanilla essence
boiling water

1. Preheat the oven to moderate (180°C). Line two baking trays with non-stick baking paper.

2. Combine the butter and water in a large saucepan, and heat until the butter melts and the mixture comes to the boil. Sift the flour into the pan, and stir with a wooden spoon over the heat for about 1 minute, until the mixture comes away from the sides of the pan in a lump.

3. Transfer the mixture to a bowl and cool slightly, stirring to release the heat. Add the eggs a little bit at a time, beating well with electric beaters between each addition, until the mixture is very thick and glossy.

4. Place the mixture into a piping bag fitted with a plain 1.5cm nozzle. Pipe into 8cm lengths, leaving room for rising and spreading. Bake for 20–25 minutes, until puffed and golden brown. Transfer to a wire rack to cool.

5. Split the éclairs lengthways, and fill with whipped cream.

6. For the icing, sift the dry ingredients together, then mix in the butter, vanilla and enough boiling water to make a smooth paste. Spread over the top of the éclairs and leave to set.

Cream buns

PREP TIME: 30 MINS + RISING
COOKING TIME: 20–25 MINS
MAKES 16

¾ cup lukewarm water
1 tbsp dry yeast
4 cups plain flour (or bread flour)
¼ cup caster sugar
¾ cup lukewarm milk
60g butter, melted
1 egg yolk
raspberry jam, to taste

MOCK CREAM
125g unsalted butter
½ cup caster sugar
1 tsp vanilla essence

NOTE: Fill with fresh whipped cream rather than mock cream, if you like.

1 Combine the water and yeast in a jug and stand for 5 minutes, or until starting to become frothy.

2 Sift the flour and sugar into a large bowl and make a well in the centre. Add the yeast mixture, milk and butter, and use a wooden spoon then your hands to mix to a soft dough. Turn out onto a lightly floured surface and knead for 8 minutes, until smooth and elastic.

3 Place the dough into a large, lightly oiled bowl. Cover with a clean tea towel and stand in a warm place for 1 hour, or until the dough has doubled in size. Punch the dough down, turn out onto a floured surface and knead briefly. Divide into 16 even portions and roll into balls.

4 Preheat the oven to hot (220°C), and grease two large baking trays. Place the dough balls onto the tray, leaving room for rising. Cover with a clean tea towel, and stand for 10 minutes.

5 Brush the top of the buns with the egg yolk lightly beaten with 2 tsp water. Bake for 10 minutes then reduce the heat to moderate (180°C) and bake a further 10–15 minutes until risen and golden brown. Transfer to a wire rack to cool.

6 To make the mock cream, use electric beaters to cream the butter, sugar and vanilla until pale. Pour cold water onto the mixture, then drain off. Beat for another 2 minutes. Repeat this 5 more times, until the mixture is very light and fluffy.

7 Make a cut in the top of each bun and fill with the mock cream. Add a dollop of jam, and serve.

Scones

My kids loved baking and were always entering competitions. When my youngest son, Robert, was eleven, he cooked some scones for the junior section of a local competition. For some reason he made an extra big batch, so he entered some in the senior section as well. Guess what? He received first prize and I came second! I've never lived it down.

Ginger scones

PREP TIME: 10 MINS
COOKING TIME: 12–15 MINS
MAKES 18

4 cups self-raising flour
pinch of salt
¾ cup cream
2 tbsp milk
60ml Buderim ginger refresher
125ml soda water
4 tbsp uncrystallised ginger, finely chopped

1. Preheat oven to hot (220°C) and lightly grease a baking tray.

2. Sift the flour and salt into a mixing bowl and make a well in the centre. Use a wooden spoon to mix in the cream, milk, ginger refresher, soda water and ginger until combined.

3. Use your hands to gather the dough together. Knead gently and briefly until smooth. Don't overwork the dough or you will have tough scones. Use a rolling pin to roll out to about 1.5cm thick. Use a 6cm round cutter to cut into 18 scones.

4. Place slightly apart on the tray and bake for 12–15 minutes, until risen and golden brown.

NOTE: Uncrystallised ginger is available in bags in the dried fruit section at the supermarket. Ginger refresher is like a ginger cordial. If you can't get it, replace it and the soda water with 185ml of ginger ale.

Scones

PREP TIME: 10 MINS
COOKING TIME: 12–15 MINS
MAKES ABOUT 15

3 cups self-raising flour
1 tsp cornflour
1 tsp baking powder
pinch of salt
2 tbsp cream
1–1¼ cups milk, plus extra to brush
jam and cream to serve

1. Preheat oven to hot (220°C) and lightly grease a baking tray.

2. Sift the flours, baking powder and salt into a mixing bowl and make a well in the centre. Use a butter knife to mix in the cream and enough milk to make a soft dough.

3. Gather the dough together and turn out onto a lightly floured bench. Knead gently and briefly until smooth. Don't overwork the dough or you will have tough scones.

4. Use a rolling pin to roll out to about 1.5cm thick. Cut out rounds with a 5cm round cutter and place slightly apart on the tray. Brush tops lightly with milk, and bake for 12–15 minutes, until risen and lightly browned.

5. Serve warm or at room temperature, with jam and cream.

Pumpkin scones

PREP TIME: 10 MINS
COOKING TIME: 12–15 MINS
MAKES 16

2 tbsp butter
¾ cup white sugar
1 egg
1 cup cold mashed pumpkin
pinch of salt
3 cups self-raising flour
1 tsp cornflour
1 tsp baking powder

NOTE: If the pumpkin is dry, add a little milk.

1 Preheat oven to hot (220°C) and lightly grease a baking tray.

2 Use electric beaters to cream the butter, sugar and egg until pale. Stir in the pumpkin and salt.

3 Sift the flours and baking powder over the mixture. Use a butter knife to mix in until evenly combined. Gather the dough together and turn out onto a lightly floured bench. Knead gently and briefly until smooth.

4 Use a rolling pin to roll out to about 2cm thick. Cut out rounds with a 5cm cutter and place slightly apart on the tray. Bake for 12–15 minutes, until risen and lightly browned.

Date scones

1. Preheat oven to hot (220°C) and lightly grease a baking tray.

2. Sift the flour, baking powder, cornflour and salt into a mixing bowl. Stir in the dates and make a well in the centre. Use a butter knife to mix in the cream and enough milk to make a soft dough.

3. Gather the dough together and turn out onto a lightly floured bench. Knead gently and briefly until smooth. Don't overwork the dough or you will have tough scones.

4. Use a rolling pin to roll out to about 1.5cm thick. Cut out rounds with a 5cm round cutter and place slightly apart on the tray. Brush tops lightly with milk, and bake for 12–15 minutes, until risen and lightly browned.

PREP TIME: 10 MINS
COOKING TIME: 12–15 MINS
MAKES 16

3 cups self-raising flour
1 tsp baking powder
1 tsp cornflour
pinch of salt
¾ cup chopped dates
2 tbsp cream
1–1¼ cups milk, plus extra to brush

Sultana scones

PREP TIME: 10 MINS
COOKING TIME: 12–15 MINS
MAKES 12

2 cups self-raising flour
2 tbsp caster sugar
1 tsp baking powder
1 tsp mixed spice
1 tsp cornflour
pinch of salt
¼ cup sultanas
1 cup thickened cream
½ cup milk, plus extra to brush

1 Preheat the oven to hot (220°C) and lightly grease a baking tray.

2 Sift the flour, sugar, baking powder, mixed spice, cornflour and salt into a mixing bowl. Stir in the sultanas and make a well in the centre. Use a butter knife to mix in the cream and milk to make a soft dough.

3 Gather the dough together and turn out onto a lightly floured bench. Knead gently and briefly until smooth. Don't overwork the dough or you will have tough scones.

4 Use a rolling pin to roll out to about 2cm thick. Cut out rounds with a 6cm round cutter and place slightly apart on the tray. Brush tops lightly with milk, and bake for 12–15 minutes, until risen and lightly browned.

Acknowledgements

I had no idea just how much work and dedication went into the preparation of this book until it all started.

First, I would like to thank Cheryl Akle, my agent, for the patience, you never faulted.

I would especially like to say a sincere thank you to the staff of Random House Australia – nothing was too much trouble to get the book completed and I am so thrilled with the result. To photographers Steve Brown and Ben Dearnley, stylist Janelle Bloom, home economists Kerrie Ray and Wendy Brodhurst, thank you so much for making this book look so beautiful. Special thanks to Tracy Rutherford for all your hard work. Trisha Garner, who designed the book, and Kerry Klinner, who typeset it – you have all done me proud. Thank you.

Special thanks go to my family: David, Lucinda, Alexander and Michael for always asking 'How's the book, Nan?'. To Marianne, Peter and Jarrett who are always there for support, and happy to have me overnight or for a week. To Robert, Kim, Nicole, Jason and Samantha, for always being there for me with encouragement.

There are many people in my extended family – far too many to name – so if I miss anyone please forgive me but you know who you are. Lyn and Ken, Margaret, Kellie, Gail and Russell, and so many others, thank you all for your foresight and encouragement. I really do appreciate your support.

To the readers of my book: I hope you get as much enjoyment out of trying my recipes as I have had making them for my family and friends over the years. Don't forget we all have failures at times!

Index

A
Anzac biscuits 100
apple
  cake 6
  pie 78
  strudel 94
arrowroot biscuit slice 160

B
banana
  cake with caramel icing 22
  caramel and banana pancakes 90
  slice 143
biscuit cake 44
biscuits/cookies
  Anzac biscuits 100
  butterscotch biscuits 121
  choc-chip cookies 114
  coconut biscuits 106
  fruit mince cookies 102
  ginger nuts 108
  jam drops 118
  melting moments 105
  Merle's honey jumbles 98
  oatmeal cookies 116
  peanut biscuits 124
  plain biscuits 110
  rock cakes 122
  shortbread 113
brownie, Mum's 184
buttercake, plain 38
buttercream icing 41
butterscotch
  biscuits 121
  rice pudding 68
  'sponge' pudding 74

C
cake/s see also sponge/s
  apple 6
  baked cheesecake 36
  banana cake with caramel icing 22
  biscuit 44
  carrot 42
  chocolate layer 10
  chocolate ripple 20
  cinnamon nut 12
  Donna Latter's chocolate 46
  lemon cheesecake 17
  lime and buttermilk 33
  melt and mix Christmas 14
  orange 25
  patty 26
  peach blossom 4
  pineapple fruit 30
  plain buttercake 38
  pumpkin fruit 9
  rainbow 18
  small 41
  speedway 28
  sultana 2
  walnut 34
caramel
  caramel and banana pancakes 90
  fingers 164
  icing 22, 164
  slice 146
carrot cake 42
cheesecake
  baked 36
  lemon 17
chocolate
  almond slice 135
  butter icing 34
  choc-chip cookies 114
  Donna Latter's chocolate cake 46
  éclairs 204
  fruit slice 162
  fudge slice 159
  layer cake 10
  ripple cake 20
  sponge 54
Christmas cake, melt and mix 14
Christmas pudding, rich 82
cinnamon nut cake 12
cinnamon sponge 60
Clyde's pudding 66
coconut
  biscuits 106
  ice 190
  slice 148
coffee icing 144
coffee walnut slice 144
cookies see biscuits/cookies
cream buns 206
cream puffs 196
crumble, peach 86
custard tarts 198